WAS IT YESTERDA

WAS IT YESTERDAY

MEMOIRS OF THE 1914-1918 WAR

A. M. BOWN

YOUCAXTON PUBLICATIONS

OXFORD & SHREWSBURY

Contents

Reviews of the 1928 edition.

"No synopsis of the movements and adventures of that battery could give an adequate impression of the scope of the book and quotation would do it less than justice. In style it is simple, light yet adequate; the humour is never forced and the ever present sense of tragedy is never unduly emphasized."
Times Literary Supplement

"Those who enjoy a vivid narrative of the war as it appeared to an artilleryman will find *Was it Yesterday?* one of the most clear stories of the war that have been written ... We delight in Major Bown's book because there is no reaching after effect, no painting in of the horror - just a true realism which every serviceman will appreciate."
The Lincolnshire Echo

"*Was it Yesterday?* by A. M. Bown belongs to the limited number of good stories of the great war. It is a plain unvarnished tale of the experience of a young artillery officer. ...As an author Mr. Bown reveals a lack of technical skill in telling his story but he has had so much vivid material at his disposal that he has produced a notable book."
The Age (Melbourne)

"His narrative is simple but very convincing. Mr. Bown has a gift for tense descriptive writing which makes his story breathless reading".
The Melbourne Argus

"Whoever wants to obtain a true idea of what trench warfare means should read *Was it Yesterday?* by A.M. Bown."
The Johannesburg Star

"If I had been sent to follow Joshua in a seven days' tramp round Jericho, I should not have been more surprised to see its brick walls totter to crumbling ruin than I was to see that mighty bulwark of Germany collapse as fatally."

The Week (Brisbane) [One of the dramatic insights in a book which never hides its respect for the enemy, in spite of the use of the words, Hun, Boche and Fritzes which were then in common use.]

A copy of *Was it Yesterday?* was sent to the Imperial War Museum library in September 1928 and can still be seen there.

This edition is dedicated to their parents
Arthur Mervyn Bown MC
and one-time Shrewsbury and Atcham Borough Councillor
Dorothy Ethel Bown,
by their surviving children Lalage, Jacqueline and Hugh

WAS IT YESTERDAY?

BY

A. M. BOWN

LONDON
JOHN HAMILTON LTD.
PUBLISHERS

Former title page

Introduction

Arthur Mervyn Bown[1] published this book, *Was it Yesterday?* in 1928. Written in novel form, the episodes ascribed to fictitious characters are drawn from his experiences in the Great War of 1914-1918. Some of them used to be related to his family over the breakfast table years later in Shropshire.

The Author in the Great War

The British ultimatum to Germany expired on 4th August 1914. On 25th August, less than a fortnight after his 20th birthday, A.M. Bown, who had then been two years at Oxford, took a commission as a 2nd Lieutenant in the 7th London Brigade, Royal Field Artillery. His name remained on the Army List until April 1919.

He served in France throughout the war, barring periods of leave and two periods of convalescence from wounds. He was on sick leave in England when the final retreat and defeat of the Germans took place. He was fortunate to have survived, since the death toll among subalterns was extremely high; the lists of names on war memorials, such as that in many Oxford and Cambridge college war memorials show this. He was promoted to acting Lieutenant in May 1917[2] and his last entry in the 1919 Army Lists shows him as full Lieutenant. Throughout the war, in Army records, his name is shown on the same page as his lifelong friend, R. B. Ullman. There also appears with them the name of Lt W. L. Bragg, later to

---

1   Born 12th August 1894. Died 14th January 1969.

2   A review of this book in the Lincolnshire Echo describes the author as "Major A.M. Bown". This could be through conjecture from internal evidence in the first chapter. His place name at regimental reunion dinners in the 1950s gave him the title of Captain which must then have been his acknowledged rank. There is no record of a higher rank in the Army Lists up to 1918. The difference could be explained by the distinction between substantive and acting ranks or it could relate to promotion during territorial service after the war.

become known as a distinguished scientist; A. M. Bown worked with him on research into sound-ranging.

There are undoubtedly more personal references to be found in the records. On 4th January 1916, Lt Ullman was "sent on a course at Gosnay". On 4th January 1916, Lt Bown "rejoined from England", presumably after recovery from one of his wounds; and then on 29th May 1917, it was noted that Lt A. M. Bown and 2nd Lt l. S. T. Davis were "slightly wounded"

He served in "C" battery of the 7th London Brigade and while the characters in his novel are described as belonging to a fictitious regiment, they also belong to "C" battery. He was assigned to the ammunition column until June 1916 when he moved into work closer to the front line. His award of the Military Cross was gazetted on 18th June 1917.

The unit war diaries of the 7th London Brigade can be found in the Public Records Office under "47th Division". The brigade was absorbed into 237th brigade Royal Field Artillery and later 237 was broken up and the 7th London personnel moved to 235 brigade. The diaries give a complete daily entry from 1915 to the end of the war. Place names most frequently mentioned in 1 915 are Auchel, Cambrin, Givenchy, Cuinchy, Noyelles, Ames, Grenay, Les Brebis, Vermelles, Cauchy-La-Tour, Sailly La Bourse. In 1916 again Sailly La Bourse, Les Brebis, and in 1917, Camblain, Bois de Bouvigny (which is given a map reference X2b55 sheet 36 C SE), Barlin, Ypres, Chateau Beige, Hill 60, Triangular Wood and Metz. Then in 1918 Ribecourt, Fremicourt, Chateau de la Haie and Bazieux. These would all be traceable on the map of north France and Belgium and identified with places mentioned in this book. In particular, Messines, Ypres and the notorious Hill 60 in the beginning of chapter V, are among places described in the book.

Three example maps of the western front are included with this reprint: the first features Givenchy, Cuinchy, Noyelles, Vermelles and Sailly La Bourse; the second Ypres and Messine; while the third more detailed map of Ypres shows the pivotal position of Hill 60.

The 7th London was, as said, a field artillery regiment[3] and artillery played a prominent role throughout the war. Fifty-eight percent of the casualties have been attributed to artillery fire. A.M. Bown and W.L. Bragg were seconded for some period to work on sound ranging, - a system in which the report from an enemy gun would be registered on two or more listening devices and the time differences recorded; from these, it was possible to calculate the position of the enemy. The technique has been described as contributing significantly to the accuracy of British artillery and British success was envied by the Germans, who had not been able to keep up with it. A..M. Bown was also seconded for some time to write two small manuals of artillery practice.

The citation for A.M. Bown's Military Cross can be found on microfiche in the Public Records Office:--

"For conspicuous gallantry and devotion to duty. During hostile shelling the ammunition in the gunpit was set on fire. He went to the pit to extinguish the fire. While thus employed a large number of trench mortar bombs exploded a short distance away wounding a man in the pit. He removed the man to a dugout and returning, succeeded in extinguishing the fire thus saving a large quantity of ammunition."

After the war, A. M. Bown went back to Oxford, passed top of his year in the entry examination for the Indian Civil Service and spent the next twenty years in India and Burma. Returning to Britain, he worked for the Scientific Instrument Manufacturers' Association and then settled down for the last 25 years of life as a farmer in Shropshire.

---

3   The illustration on the front cover is of a howitzer obtained recently from the photographic archive at the Imperial War Museum. The original cover of the book showed an artists impression of the front and is no longer useable.

The Book

Almost everyone who came back from the 1914-18 war had lived through horrors compared with which the content of the best books written in peacetime might seem mundane and dull. Because there were so many books about the war only a few get singled out as classics, some deservedly and some by chance. *Journeys End* which was first performed in the publication year of *Was it Yesterday?*, deservedly sold 175,000 copies and was translated into 24 languages. Possibly the most well-known of all was *All Quiet on the Western Front* published in the following year 1929. The author Erich Maria Remarque spent only one month at the front. Edmund Blunden who had written his own memoirs in 1928 under the title of *Undertones of War*, described Remarque's book as "piddling idle rubbish". Among powerful works deservedly recognised are memoirs by Siegfried Sassoon and Robert Graves, and the poetry of Wilfred Owen.

A. M. Bown wrote his book nearly ten years after the war ended and therefore it might be said to have been "recollected in tranquility". He was distanced enough to have a sober perspective, but without having lost the consciousness of horror and muddle, as well as of steadfast soldiering. The title, *Was It Yesterday?* is a quotation from Matthew Arnold's poem *The Forsaken Merman,* in which it is a recurring chorus to underline a sense of loss. He was attached to Arnold's poetry and sometimes used to quote from *On Dover Beach.* The two poems both give voice to sadness at the vanishing of illusion.

When his novel first appeared, it was well-received by reviewers in several countries. For example, an Australian commentator wrote: "His narrative is simple but very convincing. Mr. Bown has a gift for tense descriptive writing which makes his story breathless reading". A modern audience will value both the descriptions and the straightforward style. The book has one of the best descriptions of a dug-out and life in it, for instance. There are episodes of humour and a variety of interesting characterization including the stolid bravery of the stretcher-bearers and the determination of a Flemish peasant to finish his "piece-work", while everyone else is fleeing. It also conveys how in war conditions, soldiers become preoccupied with food. There is an amusing description of an officers' meal, which is a pastiche of a dinner of several courses, starting with Oxo soup and going on to sardines.

The book starts by describing the more relaxed days of the early part of the war, while later chapters move to horrific scenes of fighting at the front. This echoes the real-life unit's war diaries, in which the early entries deal with routine matters like route marches, attendance at lectures and visits by senior officers. The entries in 1916 and 1917 are longer and more violent, recording the use of gas-shells, the heavy bombardment on the Kaiser's birthday, the monthly table of casualties and replacements. The year 1918 starts with some of the fiercest fighting and ends quietly with matters like the registration of voters under the Representation of the People Act. But those diaries cannot convey the sense of bewilderment and disorder which ordinary soldiers experienced and which several episodes in this novel convey so graphically.

While depicting the discipline, sense of duty and certainty that Britain would win through in the end, the book also describes what many readers may find surprising, the disbelief that the war ended when it did. As the author says:

" ... if I had been sent to follow Joshua in a seven days' tramp round Jericho, I should not have been more surprised to see its brick walls totter to crumbling ruin than I was to see that mighty bulwark of Germany collapse as fatally".

Although written nearly ninety years ago, much of the book will ring true to modern ears, but obviously some of the conversational idioms of the 1920s have to be taken in context. Derogatory references to the enemy as "Boche", "Fritzes" and "Huns" are no longer acceptable in the 21st century. Nevertheless, these terms should be mitigated by the obvious respect in which the author held the people to whom, in wartime, such epithets were so easily applied.

Republication

A reprint of *Was it Yesterday?* was made in 2002 for family use with no ambitions to revive its chances of catching public imagination, but now that so much is being done to commemorate the Great War, and when indeed one of the original copies of the book has been offered at apparently a hundred times its original price, it seemed reasonable to republish it for a wider readership.

To his family, who are making arrangements for this reprint, A.M. Bown's story must have a special significance. Had a shell burst a few yards to the right, had the aim of a rifleman been a little more accurate, then some of us would never have been born. As it is we have lived our adult lives through 70 years of peace. We owe this peace to the thousands of men whose hardships are described in these pages. And turning specifically to our own parents, it is not arrogant to ask that their work should be remembered by our generation and those who come after us.

In the words of Milton:-

"Forsitan has laudes decantatumque parentis
Nomen ad exemplum sero servabitis aevo" .[4]

"Maybe this praise and celebration of a parent's name,
Could preserve it for an age to come".

H.B.

---

[4] Milton, Silvarum liber. poem address to his father. Roughly translated "And you, my verses, ... perhaps through this praise and celebration of a parent's name, you will preserve it as an example for times to come".

Acknowledgements

The Photograph on the front cover is reproduced courtesy of the Imperial War Museum, London. (Image number Q 564).

The three maps are reproduced by permission of the Western Front Association.

There were no illustrations in A.M. Bown's original 1928 publication.

Acknowledgement must also be made of the helpfulness and courtesy shown by staff of the Public Records Office and of the Imperial War Museum without which the introduction to this present edition could not have been written.

Photograph of A.M. Bown in uniform.

Field artillery pieces were horse drawn in 1914-18

"C" Battery (?). A.M. Bown on back row right.

Maps

The three maps which follow show some of the place names mentioned in *Was it Yesterday?* and in this introduction. The front line marked in each of them is shown only as an example of the position at different stages of the war.

Map 3 is a detail of map 2 and the relationship between maps 1 and 2 can be envisaged from the fact that Bethune lies approximately 25 miles south west of Ypres.

The maps are as follows:-

1. British and French positions before Bethune at the time of the German attacks on Givenchy and Cuinchy in January 1915

2. Northern flank of the allied line before the opening of the offensive July 31st 1917.

3. The Ypres salient before and after the 2nd battle of Ypres April 22nd- May 13th 1915.

Map 1

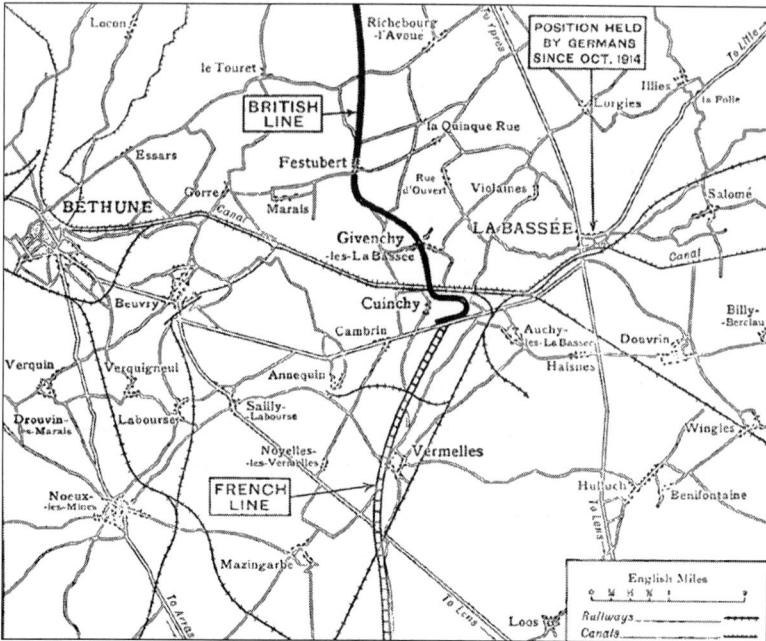

Vimy Ridge and Souchez are located at the south of the thickly marked 'British Line'. Souchez lies to the south west of Givenchy and is now the site of one of the largest war cemeteries.

Map 2

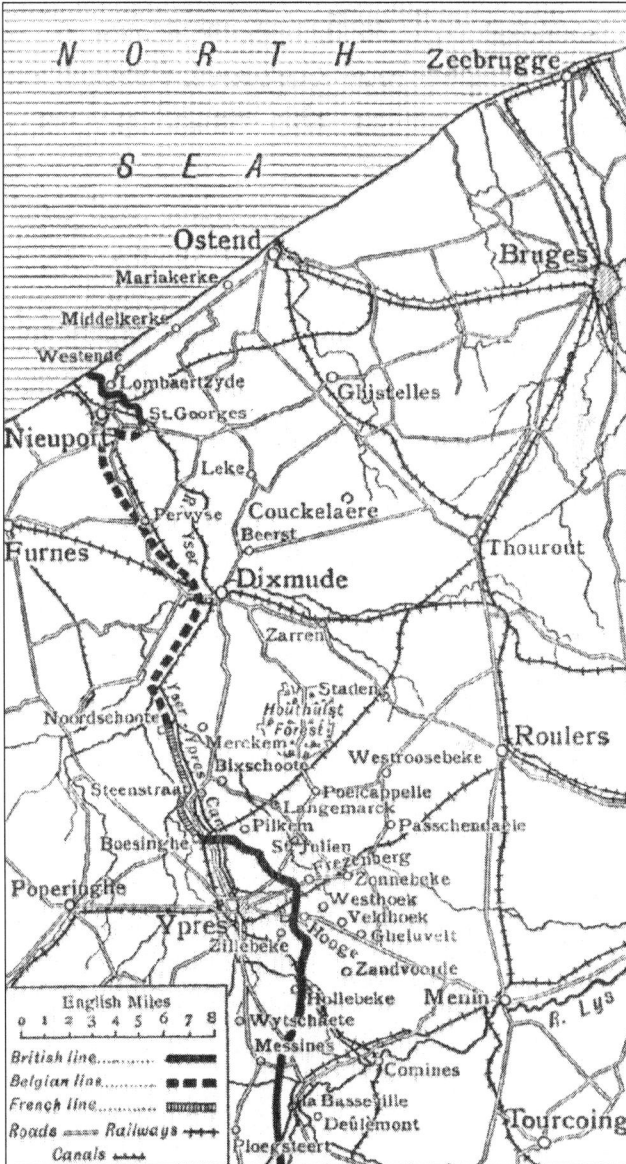

Large scale view of the Western Front showing Belgian,
British and French front lines.

Map 3

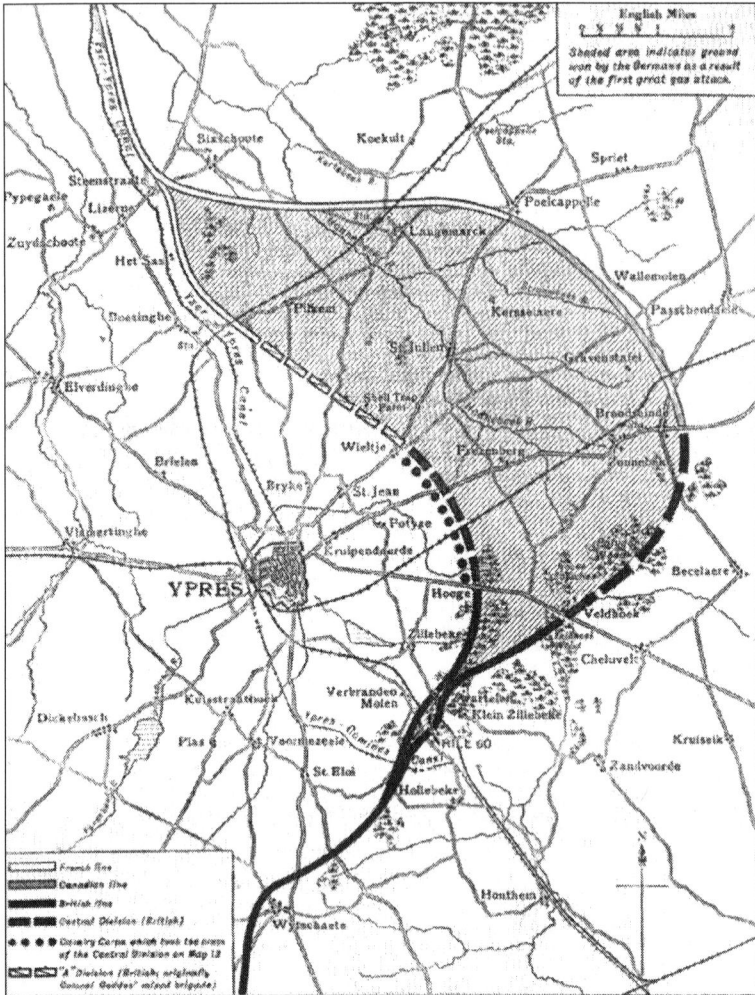

The Ypres Salient. Territory to the west of the shaded area was held by
the British through the four years from 1914.

CHAPTER I

In the Beginning.

Life in a dugout behind the front line - early days -
comparatively quiet - cynical discussion about war correspondents -
"perhaps I shall write the real story sometime".

"NEARLY eight, sir! Your tea is ready, sir!"

This meant that it was half-past seven, and the cook had lit the fire for making the Major's morning cup of tea. The Major grunted, his bed creaked, and his servant quietly collected the heap of clothes which covered the foot of the bed and took them out to clean.

"After eight, sir! Your tea is getting cold." The door of the dugout was wide open, and the frosty gleam of a keen winter's morning seemed to fight its way into the darkness within. But the kind of darkness which lurked in Flanders dugouts is not to be defeated by so simple a thing as a two-foot doorway; only a soft haze spreading inwards made it almost more difficult to see anything than it had been before the door was opened. There are different kinds of darkness - that of the coal-cellar in an old house, or the dungeons in the Tower, or a lane through a wood which has a ghost story - but perhaps no other is like the cheerful friendly darkness which lived with one in a dugout. This dugout too had a better sample of it than most; it was nearly five yards long, which was just enough for one end never to be visible from the other; it was almost eight feet wide at the floor, but the curved black sheets of iron which leaned against the one upright wall to make a combined outside wall and roof, gave that effect of narrowness essential to the best dugouts. Two stout balks used as props took up moreover just enough of the clear space to redeem this extensive apartment from an approach to cheerless vastness; as props they were singularly wasted in supporting a roof which was not strong enough to stop a whizz-bang; but one other useful purpose they did serve: to divide the dugout into just the right proportions for the seniority and amount of kit accumulated by the three gentlemen lodging there for some winter shooting.

Tucked in by the sloping wall, close by the doorway, was a wire-covered framework on which lay a heap of blankets covered with old tunics, breeches, waterproof and British Warm. From time to time a delicate wreath of condensed moisture was wafted through a bright green muffler at the head of the bed, and this was the only evidence that underneath it breathed the owner, to wit Captain John Brown, a keen enough officer when he was awake, but an infernally hard sleeper at eight o'clock in the morning. Further along, pushed in between the supporting props was a stretcher raised on two empty ammunition boxes. Not even a breath was noticeable there, for to Lieutenant Arthur Fitzroy Thurston, who occupied it, would fall the privilege of giving a lead to his senior officers when they faced the chilly prospect of getting out of bed; this rising tactician was intent on making no creak which would hasten the moment when the Major would call him to it. Across the end of the dugout enjoying the luxury of a couch, carpentered, canvas-covered and padded with sandbags, lay the officer commanding C/XYZ Battery of Royal Field Artillery, looking just now like a particularly disreputable Covent Garden porter as he sat up from amid his blankets and trench-coat with a ragged Cardigan jacket over his pyjamas, and a Balaclava helmet which his Aunt had knitted for him in two colours when khaki wool was unobtainable.

The Major looked at the steaming cup of tea on the chair at his bedside, then at his wrist-watch.

"Phizz !"

There was no answer; the quiet form on the stretcher was still more intensely quiet.

"Phizz, you must get up earlier; it's after eight now - absurd time! To-morrow you will have to——": but just in time Thurston, answering to the name of Phizz, broke in with a groan and a terrific creak of his stretcher as he turned over without rolling off: which is an acrobatic feat needing skill and experience.

"Gott strafe the war! What time is it, Major?"

"Eight, you slack young devil - in bed in the middle of the day, and a war on! I'll bet every Boche gunner in the Salient has been up hours. No wonder we don't win !" Then as he watched the play of the dim light from the door on the curling smoke of his first cigarette, he added, "Thank God we ain't Huns !"

Thurston turned over once more on to his back and bellowed for his servant.

"My shaving water, Bailey! You're infernally late this morning," he cursed, passing on the 'strafe' according to the truest traditions of the Army.

"It is here, sir." Bailey lit a couple of candles and put beside the bed an upturned box complete with shaving tackle set neatly round a centre-piece of broken mirror and flanked in careful symmetry by the two dirty candles stuck in empty whisky bottles.

"What time did the ration wagon get up last night, Bailey?"

"There are two letters for you, sir, and a parcel— looks like a cake." This cryptic answer did not conceal in code the true time of arrival of the ration cart; it was the answer to what was really in Thurston's mind camouflaged under the keen officer's eagerness with regard to supplies.

"Bills?"

"One is not, sir; the postmark's from Bedford."

"Good." And the wisdom of the Major's ruling that ' the mail ' must not be brought in, but kept for the breakfast table, was justified in the sudden perilous dash with which Thurston retrieved himself from his stretcher and set himself to getting up for breakfast and the letter from Bedford.

"Was there any mail for me, Bailey?" asked the Major.

"Don't think so, sir. Your paper was·all. But ' the Quarter ' said we'd done a push somewhere; and took ten thousand prisoners. 'E said the Navy Division had got Anker and the Germans have asked for an *armistyce*, and a blue light was goin' to be the signal, sir."

"Good Lord, Brownie; hear that?" the Major called across to the bundle of bedding beneath which still slumbered his second-in-command: "The Naval Division have crossed the Ancre and done in the Boches; there must be at least three thousand prisoners, if the quartermaster says there are ten. Pull him out of bed, Phizz, and wake the torpid old devil up!"

"What's that?" growled the sleepy voice of Brown, who 'liked to wake up slowly.' He yawned as he stretched himself' and asked if peace had been declared.

"I shouldn't be surprised. Here, Bailey, bring the paper in, and we'll see if we are winning the war."

"Oh, look here, Major, that isn't playing fair. If you get your paper, I should have my letter— I mean my letters," Phizz spluttered through his towel.

"Shut up, you insubordinate young devil. You can bring Mr. Thurston's bill in, Bailey, but not the thick one in the tinted envelope." Bailey chuckled; he had a wife and four children drawing separation allowance, but he could appreciate what letters like that meant. The Major went on, "I thought there was a lot of noise down South, but it went on too long for anything like a walk-through. Brigade said they had no news through." Bailey came in with the paper and the Major opened it.

"The R.N.D. had a great show in the morning fog, but the communique doesn't give much away. I don't expect they know much about it yet either. Well, here you are, Brownie," and he threw the paper across to Brown, who opening it glanced through the headings of the Law Reports.

When later the Major and Brown went in to breakfast, a bright wood fire was burning at the end of the mess dugout - wood 'scrounged' from wrecked houses, and some 'borrowed' from R.E.'s (who seem hardly to realise that the first value of wood is to give warmth; they get obstreperous on the subject of burning pit props for instance, so perhaps it were better to slur over any details of that cheery fire). Thurston was talking over the news with the second subaltern, Gurney, who had been up on duty that morning.

"Isn't it extraordinary that we out here, right on the spot, fighting this war—— began Phizz.

"Dashed lot of fighting you've done this morning!" said the Major, and glanced at his dutiful subaltern stretched out in a canvas chair with a cigarette in one hand, paper in the other, and his slippered feet toasting on the hearth while his field boots were warming on the other side.

"I consider it essential to the maintenance of the fighting efficiency of my battery, that the highest standard of comfort should be maintained off duty when that does not interfere with——"

(Phizz was quoting his O.C.'s words with an obstreperous Corps General who believed in 'hardening' on the Spartan model).

"Get on with your own speech, Phizz, and let mine alone. What wise revelations were you going to make about the war?"

"Well, don't you think it is rather a funny position to be here in this jolly old war, and not to know what is happening until you get the papers from home?"

"And then you find out all about it, of course," Brown interjected sarcastically. "Here is this communique: ' The situation on the left bank is not yet clear.' In other words, the infantry don't know where they are, the Staff don't know either where the infantry or the Boches are; and meanwhile gunner observation officers and aeroplanes and heaven knows what are being chivied around to find out anything at all and get a message back. We are the eyes of the Army, my boy, and don't you forget it: at least you might be if you didn't spend most of your day at O.P.[5] listening to the mess gramophone over the telephone, instead of doing what you are paid for."

Brown was getting well away with his growl and his bacon at the same time, but lost his place through dropping his toast on the carpet in the excitement, and having to pick it up.

"That is all very well, Brown," the Major broke in, "but what we see are the little bits, the tiny little pieces of this Jig-saw puzzle. We know no more than sweet Fanny Adam about the real position until the papers come out from home."

"Quite, Major; and they will have one tiny bit of communique which may mean what it says or may make an awful knock in the eye look like a young victory, with all over bar shouting. Then there will be yards and yards of War Correspondent trying to tell us what the war is like. This blank toast is dry as oats. By the way, one sack of oats was mouldy yesterday, and Supplies won't replace

---

5   "O.P." is the battery observation officer's look-out post.

it. How can the General expect the horses to be fat and fit if he won't ginger the A.S.C.?"

"Oh, cut out shop at this time of day, Brownie," Phizz broke in. "Here you are, how's this, a propos of war correspondents: ' One battalion commander told me that his men begged to be allowed to take part and almost cried when told that they would have to stay in reserve.' And here's another better still: ' The gunners stood by their beloved cannon *cannon*, mark you ! - ' putting the last touch of polish with a gentle rub of this lever or that, as they waited for the great moment when their wicked-looking' monsters would bark out their angry message of death.' Does it make you sick, or can you stick this one: ' The morning was misty and I was not quite close enough——' "

"I'll bet he wasn't," the Major grinned.

" ' Not quite close enough to see our gallant men as like hounds released from the leash they dashed eagerly towards their goal.' Now what do you learn about the War from that stuff !"

"Who wants to learn about the War? Damn fools !" Brown growled again, but less grumpily now that he too had had his breakfast.

"Oh, lots of people want to know what it's like, of course," said Phizz as he put away the offending rag.

The Major turned round. "Girls in Bedford for instance , what! But of course I know these correspondent johnnies do talk frightfully through their hats: they are bound to. They may pick up news, but they cannot see the reality of War itself as we do, who live in it and see every side of it from the rest-villages to the front line - and beyond. You know, you're in luck, my boy. When children of yours ask Daddy what he did in the Great War, you will say, ' Child, I didn't get up in time to do much myself, but I watched other people do everything that anyone ever did: ration carrying, trench digging, drilling, observing, marching, gassing, flying, tanking, and once on a time rifling: which did not. mean what you mean by the word, but in those days there was a weapon now obsolete, called a Rifle, which that rare animal the common or garden infantryman, who was not some sort of specialist, or any other '—ist" or '—er' at all, once upon a time used.' Where was I in that sentence?"

"Bravo, Major, you're going strong. War in five films, two thousand feet of magnificent descriptive imagery, free of charge! Why don't you try your hand at it?" Brown laughed.

"I may some day if I get a Blighty one, or a job on the Staff with nothing to do, instead of this life of care with idle and insubordinate young slackers for my officers."

Some years afterwards he did.

CHAPTER II

Gunners and Infantry.

Chance meeting with an infantry officer in a patisserie in Bethune - first mention of 'Minenwerfer' - Thurston decides he should get first-hand experience of conditions among the infantry.

IN the early summer of 1915, C/XYZ Battery R.F.A. were beginning to settle into that cheerily comfortable inactivity which followed the keen disappointment of Neuve Chapelle and Festubert. Possibly the General Staff may have realised at the time how small a pinprick it was that we were attempting to make in the tough hide of Germany's vast army, but if so, then at least they were remarkably successful in camouflaging what they thought. To the rest of us, glowing with anticipation of carrying the offensive with a rush back into the enemy's country, it seemed like a vital failure on the point of winning the war. So we settled back much amazed and rather unbelieving in the defeat of the very best of Britain's manhood, and we drifted into the pleasant routine of 'peace warfare.' The gorgeous weather helped the resemblance of its lighter side to a summer holiday in the country, living the truly simple life in pleasant isolation. Most of us took it just for granted and stopped thinking.

C. Battery was particularly lucky in its position. The guns were hidden in cottage gardens of a little mining village where the inhabitants cherished the half-proud, half-indignant illusion that they had twice been mercilessly bombarded by the savage Hun; had he not sent nearly a dozen shells into the village one still evening, shells as large as those which the glorious 75's spat out at the German cannon-fodder; and when France's gallant legions were struggling up Lorette ridge on an invincible tide of blood, had not the Hun wreaked an unjust revenge on this helpless village, so that one whole family was slaughtered as they sat at supper, and hardly a house but had lost a window or a tile from the roof. Phizz gathered this and more from the kindly dame in whose garden he had his flank gun, and in whose front room was the enormous bed into which he would climb later for his night's sleep. This same bed had had the honour of resting the Commandant Lavoizelle, who was so "gentle" and so proud of his wonderful 75's. In fact Madame was just a little hurt that she should have as his successor one who was but a lieutenant and had not even been *decoré*. But she softened when she found that he could answer her voluble French fairly satisfactorily, and did not, for instance, counter her enquiries as to whether the *draps* were sufficiently *propres* with an energetic *Non Non*. And when next morning she sent him in a cup of coffee and a thin tartine, he discovered how one's personal comfort is increased by the intelligent interjection of Oui Oui ! and Non Non ! in the right places.

Phizz found the same restfulness everywhere about the war. Sir John French not only was kind enough to take the responsibility of feeding and lodging him, but provided him with just the right amount to do to keep interested and fit: and allowed just the right number of shells each day to maintain his keenness in shooting, even though for weeks there were only empty houses and quiet trenches to shoot at. The Observation Post itself was the open window of a little attic bedroom of the mining village on the forward slope: where he sat in a looted wicker chair, with the telephonists at the other side of a small table with the map spread on it. And here there was another Madame (who lived below and slept with her husband and children in the cellar on account of the stray bullets and occasional shrapnel)— who would cook him a tasty meal for his lunch and give him coffee too. But she was not so friendly as the lady of his billet; for already was the rumour that these English were not going to permit civilians to stay so close as twelve hundred yards from the German front line, but were going to insist on evacuating them: and too, the British were so foolhardy as to stir up the Boche to retaliate on this hillside village, and the place was not so safe as when their own gallant troops had wisely saved themselves and everybody else annoyance by keeping quiet at these times when they could do no earthly good by being anything else.

On those days when he was not needed at the battery nor at O.P., Phizz would ride over to the wagon-line to see his drivers and their teams, and look over the harness. Then he would ride on to Bethune and have a hot bath, and buy useless things from the jolly little French shops where the sparkling Ma'mselles had not yet learned the fatally fluent English which went hand in hand with the canker and corruption of the war zone as the years dragged on. Then there was tea at the Paon d'Or, or at the Patisserie in 'Bond Street,' and a quiet jog home in the evening.

It was at the Patisserie itself that the great adventure was conceived. Phizz was alone for tea; he walked round the shop with his ample plate, picking only those subtle creamy things which slip away so easily, and when offset by a few thicker chocolate meringues just go and leave only a general feeling of satisfaction with unspoiled desire for more. Louise brought him his tea, hot and refreshing, and settled him in the quiet corner by the window of the little back room. Now not the least discovery of Louise's genius was that if only the pastries are uniformly excellent, no man on earth can remember just how many he has eaten, and so to be on the safe side everyone guesses a number which will more than cover his actual feast, and pays accordingly. But Phizz had passed the critical point and reached the stage when, while blissfully ignorant of how many it really had been, he knew only that for very shame he could not admit to a single one more. Why had he not counted them at first! — but no one ever did. Why did not Louise count them herself! — because she was Louise. Could he see someone he knew who had eaten comparatively few and would let him lighten the guilt by sharing it? There was no one, but Phizz had noticed that the Fusilier at the next table had had very few. He plunged.

"I say, are you ready for a cigarette?"

"What?—oh, thanks very much," the stranger answered as he noticed the cigarette case held out to him. He pulled his chair closer as he took a light from the match Phizz had struck.

"I wonder if you mind my asking you," Phizz went on, "but how many cakes have you had?"

"Oh, I think only two, three will cover it, I'm sure. Why?" the infantryman asked smiling.

Phizz explained that he had had so many that he would like to join with the other in paying for eighteen or twenty, and separate the indebtedness afterwards.

"Oh rather," laughed the Fusilier, and continued: "we always overeat frightfully here too. But the other fellow, the man I usually come with when we get out of the line, was done in two nights ago, just before our relief; so I had to come alone to-day."

He spoke entirely as of a simple matter of fact; though to Phizz, who had only seen death through field glasses, and then not that of his own friends, it seemed rather dubious that one should joy-ride at all when a close companion had so recently been killed. The infantryman went on, "we had rather a bad time, this spell in the line. There was a lot of machine-gunning of our working parties out wiring at night, and we haven't anything like enough to answer them with. The Hun had lots of these minenwerfer things too; you know how rotten they are, don't you? — oh, I didn't notice you were a gunner." Phizz looked down; half serious banter from an infantryman about the soft life gunners were leading was one thing, but the entirely natural and unintentional taunt which these words carried was different. He was a gunner: and he did not know how rotten minenwerfer were.

The other politely switched on to more common ground, "These Boche 5.9 batteries are pretty hot stuff; do you ever try to stop them firing?" Phizz did not like to admit that he had only shot at enemy trenches and infantry. After all, his battery had not been shot at either, so our gunners were not worse than the Germans. "Do you think our guns do him as much damage as his crumps do to us?" the infantryman .continued. He was genuinely interested, that was clear. But Phizz had not himself experienced any damage from the Boche 5.9 inch 'crumps,' and could only make the not very flattering comparison of our own puffs of shrapnel, against the solid black bursts which shot up from our trenches when the Hun was strafing them with high explosive: so he let the infantryman go on talking.

The man was a good talker, and without striving for effect he eased his lack of companionship during the afternoon by an interesting description of his part of the line — of the water-logged breastworks at Laventie, and the single layer of sandbags over two sheets of corrugated iron which had been his last company headquarters, billet and mess, until it was knocked in on top of the mid-day meal and abandoned in favour of the open trench. At the end of his cigarette Phizz got up and settled the bill and their joint shares in it, then disappeared to find his horses. His companion of tea-time also set off to walk home.

Phizz was by now impressed with this ; that it was quite time he went down to the trenches to see the people his battery was supposed to be covering. But it did not prove so simple a thing to fit in with the leisurely battery routine. He could not leave the Observation Post when he was there — that would have been a serious crime against Army convention. He could not go when he was on duty with the guns. He was not enthusiast enough to sacrifice his day off duty by trekking up to the front line.

One evening at dinner the Major was speaking of the O.C. of another . battery. "Old Bateman is trying hard for that D.S.O. he expects to get. He works those men of his on spit-and-polish until they have no keenness for anything else, and no energy left in reserve at all. And just now he is telephoning to everyone he can think of about the tour he did yesterday in the Front Line. I'll bet the main thing he did was stop at every headquarters for a drink. But he is starting a new hare now, and suggesting that a gunner should go down to infantry each day and see what targets they wanted knocked out."

"As if his battery had ever hit any target they tried to shoot at!" Brown interjected.

The Major laughed. "Well, in any case it is a darned good advertisement. But if the only way to get a bit of ribbon is to go looking for trouble in the front line, running your head into danger when there is absolutely no necessity for it, then I know one who is not competing."

"Wouldn't it be rather good fun, Major, to buzz around the front line and have a look at things— if we cut out the advertising stunt and just did it on our own?" Phizz suggested diffidently.

"Hullo, Phizz, are you going in for the death or glory business, after promising your girl when you wept good-bye that you would be so very careful, boo-hoo? You haven't quarrelled yet or anything, have you?"

"No, Major, joking apart, we are having a very soft time here, and the infantry do pull our legs about it. I thought it might be jolly interesting to see a bit of the trenches."

The Major smiled. "There's nothing in it, Phizz; all the gunners in the Salient do their observation from the front line, and live there with the infantry. When our turn comes we shall do the same, naturally; but there is no point in going into comparative danger unless there is something to be got by it. When there is, you will be sent up there only more than you want."

"I know, Major, but still I haven't ever been in the front line; while you did that wire-cutting from the trenches up at Festubert, so it is not quite the same for you. If you don't mind, I would like to wander around the line some morning."

"Right-ho, Phizz," the Major agreed with a rather unexpected readiness; "if you like we will do a little

Cook's tour to-morrow."

And so next morning they set out with a pocketful of sandwiches for their joy-trip. As they went down the trench out of the hillside mining village not a gun was firing: only occasionally the sharp crack of a rifle told of keen eyes watching over the apparently empty plain below. On the way down they met two or three chalk-smeared infantrymen with water-bottles hung all round them, going back to the village for water; these fatigue men would flatten themselves against the trench wall to let them pass, then go slowly on disinterestedly. Occasionally they could just glimpse over the top of the parapet the deserted .houses of a village corresponding to the one they had left, but in the Boche lines. At a convenient bend they stopped under cover of the trench wall and looked back towards their own O.P. Both pulled out their field glasses and tried to make out their own observation window, and to see if it showed any sign which would betray it to a German looking there for suspicious indications.

"I beg your pardon, sir," an infantry subaltern was saluting the Major as he interrupted them; "would you mind telling me who you are?"

"Good morning. I am the battery commander of C Battery, covering this front. I am looking round the lines and stopped to observe my own O.P. to find how much of it the Germans can see. Why, are you interested?"

"Oh, I am sorry, sir, but two officers in the trenches dressed as gunners and looking through field glasses at our own lines, seemed rather odd; and you have no runner with you. But I am quite satisfied, thanks very much. Good morning, sir." He saluted and left them.

"The infantry don't exactly welcome us with flags waving, band playing and so on, do they, Phizz?" the Major remarked as they went on down the trench.

Whizz-bang, whizz-bang — two small high explosive shells burst on the trench near the village. "That must have been a near thing for the inquisitive infanteer," he added, glancing back at the thin patches of smoke drifting across the line of houses.

Before long the sandy walls of the communication trench were replaced by crumbling chalk, and just beyond this it ended in a narrower trench crossing the direction they had been going in. The parapet of the trench they had come down was generally topped with grass, occasionally buried under the loose earth thrown out of the bottom during repair work; here the parapet was sandbagged and hammered flat, showing only the smooth greasy surface of a mixture of wet brown earth and dirty chalk oozing through half-bleached sacking. The low fire-step, and the tops of a staked wire entanglement in front of the parapet misled Phizz into thinking this was the front line. Standing or sitting about in the trench were several men methodically rubbing an oily rag over well-kept rifles, or wiping cartridges from their sling bandoliers. There were eight or ten of them in a bay of about twenty yards. With elaborate unconcern Phizz was contriving to keep his head pretty low.

Having no trench-map of our own lines, the Major asked a lance-corporal which was the way forward. Whizz-bang, whizz-bang! Two more rounds shot past again to burst higher up the communication trench. Each of the infantrymen ducked, the corporal too, but without interrupting his answer. Phizz did not duck, and began therefore to feel bucked with himself. The two officers pushed slowly down a couple of bays of this support line, and so reached the continuation of the communication trench. Soon they came to the end, this time really in the front line. It was very like the support line they had just left: a little wider, the parapet rather more irregular and untidy, but yet it was just as cleanly kept and solid as the other. Somewhat fewer men seemed to be manning it, but that might only have been an impression due to its greater width. The men were even less occupied, speaking but occasionally; one was reading a soiled and crumpled letter: another was sharing a stick of chocolate with a chum: one stood with his rifle against the trench wall, and his eyes idly fixed on the bottom of a long oblong box set up against the parapet.

"This is the front line, isn't it?" the Major asked one of the men. "Sir?"

The Major altered his question. "What part of the line is this?"

"Couldn't say, sir. 'The officer ' has just gone down there, sir, if you would like to see him."

Before they went on Phizz asked where the German line ran.

"Just in front, sir, about three hundred yards. There's a periscope here, sir" — he pointed to the oblong box — "but you can't see much through it." He moved slightly to one side and pointed over the top to a desolate-looking ridge of black slag and dirt, the crest of which showed up some distance to the left. "Fritz shoots from there at night, sir, something cruel. You have to keep pretty low hereabouts after sundown or he gets you for a cert. He got two men the night before last, just here, sir. Private Whiffin, he got one right clean through the head; that's his blood there, sir," he added, almost with a touch of admiration for the Boche marksmanship as he touched a spattered stain on the chalk.

Phizz looked gingerly at the sinister slag heap, recognising it now as the end of the 'Double Crassier'; he was half expecting it to break out into sudden activity, hardly able to think that the dull silent heap of waste was not alive with hidden Germans.

Cr-r-ack! a rifle spat out. Phizz ducked hard.

The infantryman, in perfect consciousness of safety from rifle bullets at that hour, merely speculated on how many hundreds of yards further south the shot had gone. Looking warily south, Phizz thought he recognised a huge mine building with its skeleton winding tower and loose iron plates flapping slowly in the wind. "Isn't that the big mine-shaft just inside the German lines?" he asked.

"Fritz is out here, sir"; the infantryman again indicated the front. For him there were German lines only in the direction from which he got shot at. "Would you like to see through the periscope, sir?" he turned and asked the Major, who had not been trying to find Boches where no man with any sense would look for them. The Major put his glasses to the bottom of the periscope, and was looking over the waste of No Man's Land. Some twenty yards ahead was the beginning of a tangled belt of barbed wire, netted and looped on low wooden stakes; beyond was green field, with one or two occasional bare splashes where a chance shell-hole was hidden. A very slight crest about two hundred yards ahead was just enough to hide the actual Boche front line, but the enemy support trenches on the forward slope behind it lay clearly outlined by their bulky parapets of chalk. After Phizz too had looked through the periscope, the Major and he pushed along the trench towards the Double Crassier.

They chatted to the infantry, who answered respectfully but without much interest, and even with a sort of reluctance at interruption of their settled dullness. However, soon a certain comparative alertness began to infect them, which Phizz did not at first connect with a dull thud, almost too soft for any burst, followed by a long drawn out swishing as of a heavy rain falling on soft earth. They went on, and their attention was caught by the sharp blowing of a whistle; as they paused to see what it meant, again they heard the dull thud, but closer than before, and it was followed by the clatter of heavy lumps of earth raining down around them and then the lighter grit and dust which got into their teeth.

A sergeant pushed past them quickly, clearing his way with a call of "Gangway!" As he went by he called to the men manning the bay, "Minnie working. this way, clear up a bit." They took their rifles and without haste were moving up the trench. One of them as he went past spoke aloud for these strange officers to hear, but without apparently interesting himself in them or actually addressing them ; "That blessed minenwerfer will be along here next; she's hot stuff too, she is!" Now 'minenwerfer' then, when the infantry had no means of retaliation at all, but had to sit for these inventions of the evil one to lob easily in from above and just blow the trench and its unfortunate occupants into a sadly flattened heap of debris — well, minenwerfer then was an evil-sounding word. But as the gunners hesitated about pushing on or confessing to themselves that they would do better to retreat, the whistle blew again. Both looked up: Phizz's keen eyesight first caught a bloated black sausage turning heavily over in its flight as it rose quickly from the direction of the Crassier: it poised in the air, then clumsily it seemed to mark him down and with increasing speed and directness made for him as he gazed up fascinated. A rifle cracked sharply, and both ducked: it was only the chance shot of someone trying to burst the minnie in the air, but both the gunners having ducked, remained crouching in the bottom of the bay. Time stood still for one colossal instant, during which Phizz neither felt nor breathed nor thought at all, but only waited. A dull explosion shook their bay, a sweet but foul odour spread over them in a tangible smoke, and the earth and chalk and mud clattered down on top of them and died into a fine shower of dust.

"Pass the word down for stretcher-bearers! Pass it down!" a clear voice reached them from over the buttress which ended the bay they had just left. Both pushed towards the denser smoke which still poured past it. A quiet inarticulate moan carrying no voice of pain, but only weariness, reached them.

One still form showing no wound or blood at all, was that of the man who had wished to warn them of their danger.

"There is nothing we can do, Phizz "; the Major had seen that help was not needed now: only a bearer party. They turned again and went quickly down the trench once more. They passed only a couple of sentries, watching towards the Double Crassier for the next minnie, which did not come. Then they reached the end of another communication trench coming into the front line. It was also the end of the company sector, and an officer of the neighbouring company was standing there.

He saluted leisurely. "Good morning, sir. The Hun has been knocking the line about up there, hasn't he? Has he done much damage?"

"Not very much," answered the Major; "he dropped one in a bay and caught one of the fellows in it. The trench is pretty well packed now, so we thought of trying to get back up this one."

The subaltern smiled. "I wouldn't advise you to, sir, it is in a pretty bad state, and the Hun can see you from somewhere if you go up by day, and he always tries a shot."

"Rifle sniping?"

"No, not often; but those damned fizz-bang things, and they do a lot of damage too. He shoots with a 'fixed rifle' at night though, and machine-guns as well. Those minnies of his have smashed our wire about badly, and each night we try to repair it he gets at us. He overlooks us from the Crassier, you see, and what with that and his artillery, he nearly always gets somebody. It is my turn to go out to-night, so I hope he will be fairly quiet. Why is it, sir, that his artillery are so much more active at night than ours? You hardly ever seem to fire except for an S.O.S. Is it more difficult at night?"

The Major explained some of the special difficulties of night firing, but the subaltern opined that he had never noticed any inaccuracy about the enemy night fire, so perhaps they had found out more about the night conditions. He then borrowed a periscope from one of his men, and showed the Major his bit of No Man's Land — a desolate hollow strewn with tangled wire, dominated by the Double Crassier. The Boche parapet, guarded by a clean thick belt of entanglement, showed up clearly. When Phizz took the periscope he thrust it up too high for the infantryman's fancy; he was just warning Phizz when with a loud crack a bullet cut off a splinter from the wooden side. Phizz slowly got up from the bottom of the trench, still wondering if he was hurt.

"It is no use trying again here, or he will have it for sure with his next. Come further along." They moved down several yards, and Phizz looked cautiously through a fixed periscope in the next bay. The infantry officer then invited them to have lunch at his company headquarters, where they would find his O.C.; he could not come himself, being on duty until two, but they would certainly be welcome. The Major declined, however, and they decided to try the communication trench which they were standing near. "Did you notice, Major, how those infantry ducked like the devil from a whizz-bang, and stood without a wink for rifle shots? I don't mind the shells at all myself, but I can't stand that wicked crack of a Hun rifle."

"No, nor of our own, Phizz," the Major grinned, thinking of the way they had both ducked to the shot from our own trenches at the Boche minnie. "However, don't be too sure of the shells, until we are clear of this rotten trench." They were creeping along it bent nearly double to keep below the shallow parapet, and where it had been knocked partly in by a shell they almost had to grovel. The bottom was soft earth fallen in from the sides, and the going was bad. At last they reached a point where exposure was impossible to avoid, as the trench turned up the slope of another low slag heap.

"How shall you take it, Major: steadily, or a rush?"

"Oh, quietly I think. There is less chance of catching the Boche's eye then."

They crawled steadily round. Both were well clear when a single shot buried itself in the side of the slag heap behind them, throwing up a lurid cloud of ignited coal-dust.

"Steady does it, Phizz," the Major muttered, and stopped for a moment. Another round banged past to burst a hundred yards or so ahead; then after a couple of minutes another followed well up the trench. "Thank God the Hun has no imagination: he always plays the same tricks wherever he is."

Now they went on more easily, for the trench though just as soft underfoot was deeper, and they could walk upright. Near the edge of the village they decided to bolt across to it alongside a low hedge, as it would save them some long distance of tramping round. Just as Phizz followed the Major into the cover of the first house, he once again ducked hard at the report of a long range sniping shot, followed by the sizzle of a tired bullet which spat into the ground behind him. The Major cursed, for he had expected to get across unobserved and without drawing fire; but no artillery observer had noticed them, or thought them worth a round, and in the deep trench which threaded the regular lines of houses they reached their O.P. Here they settled down to lunch with Gurney, who was manning it, and afterwards followed out through field glasses the route they had taken. No Man's Land and the front line looked surprisingly different and more real after this closer acquaintance with it; and the entire absence of visible life or motion seemed unbelievable to Phizz by contrast with his recent experience of the intensity of life and sudden death which the dreary empty plain concealed. So they chatted and smoked for some time, and then left for the battery position.

"Hallo, Major, you've put your foot in it properly!" Brown greeted them as he came in to tea and found them already settled down to the table —with its clean white cloth and bowl of roses from Madame's garden.

"Well, keep the sad details till after tea," rejoined the Major, pouring out another cup and carving himself a thick slice of cake at the same time.

"Oh, it's far too urgent," Brown was searching the untidy litter of papers on the sideboard. He brought across a pink message slip and put it over the Major's plate. That worthy gentleman gulped and nearly choked himself with a sudden bellow of laughter, as he pushed it across to Phizz.

"T.Z. 1047 Date 7th. AAA Urgent AAA Battalion H.Q. report two suspicious individuals dressed as artillery officers one lean and sallow one fair hair blue eyes in trenches in front of Maroc AAA keep look out for suspicious individuals and report immediately if any of your officers are believed to be responsible AAA."

The Major rang up his Colonel at once and got the following extra details. The suspects had asked many curious questions, had behaved in an extraordinary manner, and had been followed throughout with enemy activity, especially minenwerfer. Why enemy agents should be expected to arrange to be fired on wherever they went was not explained. The Colonel laughed over the joke, but said he hoped the Major had not been running too much risk. "We don't want to lose field officers you know, in the present circumstances, and this mustn't get into a habit. Well, I'm glad you are back all right, and I will rag the infantry Colonel thoroughly about it. Goodbye."

After the amusement had died away, Phizz sat quietly thinking over the day's events; then he settled down to write to 'a girl he knew.' In the middle of it he turned and spoke.

"Thank the Lord I'm not a foot-slogger!"

"Same here, Phizz," said Brown; "an infernally dull existence with a rotten high price for excitement when you do get it," he went on, with his mind casting back to the costly battle of the Spring.

"And damnably dangerous all the time, too," Phizz added.

"Yes, Phizz, but don't congratulate yourself too much on that score. The war isn't over yet, and things are changing already. Before you've finished, my boy, the gunners won't be writing home to say how safe they are. You wait and see!"

Phizz smiled.

CHAPTER III

Counterbattery.

"Frightfulness is a game two can play at" - hitherto British and German
artillery had fired at German and British infantry;
now they discovered "counterbattery" and fired at each other.

"I WONDER if it would be safe, Major. I really think it might be."

"No, Phizz, I doubt it very much. There is one grave at least
down there, just by the edge of the stream, and there may be many
more unmarked. It would be jolly good if it were safe, but the risk
isn't worth it."

"What a pity we can't think of some way to make it safe! I hate
having to lose such a chance."

The Major and Phizz were standing on the bank of the stream
which runs through the mining village of Vermelles. North of

the village it spreads into a miniature lake with fairly deep banks, before wandering on into the marshy ground where it is lost in a series of artificial drains. Cut into the bank was a regular line of gun pits and dugouts, with high roofs clearly outlined above the ground level, for these were days before the science of counter-battery work had made concealment from the air so vitally necessary. The two officers were strolling alongside the stream smoking after the usual tea with Mr. Tickler's inevitable plum and apple, and no cake from home to relieve the monotony of it. So they were looking with some envy at the appetising fresh green beds of watercress which spread so temptingly over their little lake. But the risk of eating green food from such germ-infested waters was too great, and with a sigh of resignation they strolled on.

"This is quite a nice position, isn't it," said the Major as they turned back towards it on coming to an old wire entanglement.

"Top-hole!" Phizz agreed. "It is jolly comfortable, though I don't think much of the fellow who built our mess. Why on earth did he pack the roof with straw?"

"Oh, that is the French idea of keeping the warmth in."

"Then I wish he had not used the straw unthrashed. I don't mind mice in reason, but having a whole colony living in your roof is a bit beyond the limit. Bailey caught thirty-three yesterday in that one trap of his."

The Major laughed. "Yes, we shall have to make a·new roof as soon as we have time. This job keeps us so busy shooting though."

For months the battery had been starved of ammunition, cut down at one time to four rounds a day, with no high explosive at all, and with shrapnel shell so defective that some batteries preferred to bury even that paltry ration, rather than fire rounds which so often burst prematurely behind our own infantry.

But now at last the battery was on special duty, to engage and harass enemy artillery, with carte blanche to fire as many rounds as they liked, including wonder of wonders - the generous allowance of twenty-five per cent. high explosive. Compared with counter-battery work, as it was to develop before the end of the war, it may sound now ludicrously like pea-shooting with pop-guns; then it was a first step, and it seemed like the beginning of really being able to smash the way through to Berlin.

"You seem pleased about it, Phizz!" The Major smiled, but he spoke drily.

"Pleased? Yes, I should say so!" Phizz answered heartily "It is so jolly interesting, and the men's shooting is improving wonderfully. Don't you like it too, Major?"

The older man turned and looked at Phizz. "Well, my boy, you heard Colonel Dixon say the other day that he and his adjutant were now the only two survivors of his battalion of infantry as they came out originally. Since we came out we in the battery have had two casualties, and those only to telephonists at O.P."

"Yes, I see what you mean," Phizz said as the Major paused.

"Frightfulness is a game two can play at, and though we are starting this deliberate strafing of batteries, that does not in itself say that we shall come off best at it. The Hun has heavier stuff available than we have; and at present, better gunners.

Within a year, Phizz, we shall be taking our fair share of strafing with the P.B.I.[6]"

"And you think we shall get the worst of it, Major?"

"Not at all. I think our fellows are better men, and they will pull it off in the long run. They are a dashed good crowd," he continued, and his thoughts went to his own men; "these cheery little cockneys not one I would lose if I could have a free choice of another for him. They'll beat Fritz every time if only they get a fair chance. Good Lord!" he broke off short.

---

6   P.B.I. is trench slang for the infantry ("the poor bally Infantry." or something like that).

The two officers shed their momentary seriousness and laughed outright at the ludicrous sight in front of them. A fat little bombardier was trotting along the bank towards them pulling on one end of a string, which was tied at the other end to the leg of a terrified hen. The wretched fowl fluttered in a series of agitated dashes, protesting indignantly, until at last her breaking voice failed altogether and she allowed herself to be dragged on as a passive resister. As he passed, the bombardier saluted.

"Smithson, what are you doing?" asked the Major.

"B sub's chicken, sir! Mr. Thurston suggested exercise for it."

Phizz gasped, and the Major tactfully dismissed the bombardier, who saluted again and marched briskly on, while the hen made a determined attempt to entangle herself around the Major's leg, a contretemps only avoided by rather more agility than dignity on his part.

"What a priceless humorist you are, Phizz!" laughed the Major. "However did you manage to pull their legs like that - including the hen's?"

"I'm as innocent as a new-born—er, chicken," he grinned as he answered. "The other day I was chatting with some of the B sub-section men, and they said they thought of buying a chicken, and asked me how it should be fed. I told them, and said she would need some sort of a run for exercise if they wanted her for eggs and not for fattening. I suppose that cockney as they are, they think a hen should be exercised just as we do the horses."

"Well, I'll give you ten to one against an egg this month. Hallo, he's coming back now; we had better keep clear."

They stepped off the top of the bank and watched Smithson making his way back to the battery at a more leisurely pace. "She's going better this way, sir," he said as they smiled up at him and looked at the fluttering hen now doing her best to ease the pull on her leg instead of resisting it. Near the gun pits the bombardier stopped and led the wretched fowl down to the stream for a drink:

seeing something at last which she did understand she gulped down a drink and then cackled defiantly. The Major roared with laughter like a schoolboy.

Sw-i-sh—whong—whong! The laughter was broken short by two vicious bursts of shrapnel, which sprayed the far bank of the stream.

"Time we went in, Phizz, I think," said the Major. Then looking across to the gun pits, he added quickly, "Now what are those fools doing?" The worthy Smithson had ducked at the sound of the shells, and for an instant had let his precious charge go. Away she had scooted across the field, and the whole of B sub., who had come out to look at these unexpected shell-bursts, were now streaming across ,the old shell-holes and entanglements and trenches to recapture the fugitive.

Sw-i-sh, whong! Short of the battery this time, and dangerously close to the hen-hunt.

"Battery, Action!" a shout rang out from the telephone dugout. But just in time the sergeant, who was leading, had seized the string trailing behind the scurrying bird, and cramming her bodily into his pocket, he doubled back with his detachment to his gun pit. Orders were being shouted out, and as the Major and Phizz reached the guns they were barking out their answer to the challenge which had been flung at them. The two officers walked behind the line of pits, and reaching B sub-section, Major Osborne called to the sergeant.

"I say, Piggott, you will have to eat that hen; we can't have men wandering about the position unnecessarily now this sort of thing has started."

"Yes, sir," Sergeant Piggott answered, "I was thinking myself it will be better to make sure of her now." The hen in his pocket squawked a protest.

At that moment a signaller ran up." Mr. Gurney would like to speak to you, sir, from O.P."

The Major left Phizz at the gun pits, but very shortly called him over to the mess dugout, where by the light of a hanging lamp -

"scrounged" from an abandoned house in the village - he was ruling out lines across a large scale map.

"Gurney says he spotted the battery firing at us just now. He saw the flash twenty degrees left of La Bassée church, along this line: and thinks it is in the canal bank; but these rounds which he has just fired seemed to be short of the position. It is getting dark for observing the shells, and our own flashes will show up so well, that I didn't think it was worth while his going on, and Gurney is packing up at O.P. now and coming in. We will just wait to retaliate on this line and range if the Boche opens on us again. You see there is no enemy position marked on this map anywhere near there, but when you are up at O.P. tomorrow, you might keep a special eye open for him. Dash those mice!" One of the colony which shared the dugout with them had scratched down a shower of earth on his head.

A couple of gunners were working a compression pump clearing away the day's accumulation of water from below the plank flooring of the mess; as the Major stopped speaking, there was a swishing overhead, hardly distinguishable from the squelch of water in the pump.

"Was it?" the Major looked at Phizz and asked.

"I heard no bursts."

"They may have dudded in the marsh at the back. Look outside, will you, Phizz, and give them just a salvo if they are beginning again."

Phizz went outside, where it was now quite dark.

Another stream of some twenty shells in very quick succession seemed to brush past his head, and they all buried themselves in the mud behind. His own experience at O.P. and in the trenches had accustomed him to shelling, but to the battery it was a new development in the war. By the lights shining through dugout doorways he could see men looking out towards where the shells had wasted themselves; and he could hear some of them bantering each other under this new experience. He decided to walk down, and give orders himself as he went along for a salvo in reply.

"Fritz was very near that time wasn't he sir?" a man asked at the first pit.

"A good two hundred yards away, I think. This is rather a fine position, isn't it, to have mud all round so that the shells won't burst on it." Phizz finished his sentence just as another series whizzed over and some shrapnel bursting overhead supplied the full-stop. "We must have worried the Boche pretty considerably, to be hated like this. Get ready for a salvo to give him back."

Phizz strolled down unconcernedly giving the orders to each gun. There seemed to be nothing to worry about in this shelling which was missing them so consistently, if only by a small margin. The gunners, who had naturally less appreciation of what this retaliation meant, were rather more tense than usual, but considering that this was their first shelling they took it really very coolly. Near the end of the position Phizz noticed the two cooks in their rickety corrugated iron shelter fully engaged on getting ready a late tea; and with their minds so occupied they were the least interested in the shelling of any men on the position.

"All ready? One salvo!"

"Whoa, stop!" a voice cried from the inky darkness beyond the twinkling aiming lights set up in front of the guns. But that shout was too much for the layer of one gun, waiting tensely for the order to fire, his hand itching on the trigger with the delicacy of poise needed if a battery salvo is to be instantaneous. Bang! and the screech of the shell drowned the terrified whinnying of a horse.

"Unload!" Phizz called, and pulling out of his pocket a torch, he ran out in front of the guns. Men of the detachments were going out too, but with his mind on the enemy shelling, Phizz ordered them back to the pits, taking only Sergeant Piggott with him. The jingling of harness, the snorting of horses and the curses of the drivers mingling with it soon told him what was the matter. The ammunition wagons had come up across the front of the battery. Nobody was hurt, and the corporal in charge said he had thought it was safe as he had never known the battery to fire at night for months previously. Phizz cursed the men more or less mildly, and ordered them to drive on. But the loaded wagons had sunk in the soft mud, and the horses were terrified of that flash which had leapt up at them from in front with so agonising a roar. They jibbed and the wagons were stuck. It began to rain. Another burst of shells echoed, and shrapnel bullets splashed somewhere in the darkness, very close behind.

"Dismount all drivers and stand to your horses ! Piggott, turn out all gunners to unload. Anyone hit?

There were some murmurs to the effect of "Not yet."

As more gunners came up splashing through the mud, Phizz set them to unload steadily: there must be no risk of flurry in this first shelling. Phizz told the sergeants that the Boche was dropping his range now, and the next rounds would certainly be short of them: he expected they would from his experience of the unimaginative Boche's methods, but still he waited most anxiously for that next burst of shells. The unloading went on; gunners plunging through mud a foot deep, burdened with the heavy shells: drivers stamping their chilled feet by the side of their sweating teams: the cold drizzling rain, and pitch darkness made more intense by the flashing of an occasional torch: blasphemous men relieving their minds as they stumbled over loose trench boards and wire: and then another screech of shells, and the whine of shrapnel.

"Thank you!" Phizz muttered; the shells were short. It had been the most anxious moment he had yet had.

Interminable the time seemed before unloading was finished. The rain was heavier: the trampled mud was worse: another series of shells dropped short. Horses were whinnying at each of the continued short bursts; but at last they could turn and go. There was only a very narrow space in which the wagons could turn, and Phizz put an N.C.O. with a lantern to mark the edge of where they could go without falling into an old water-logged trench.

"Mount!" The drivers scrambled up, gathering the reins in numbed fingers. Straining at the empty wagon sunk as it was to the axles in the soft earth, the leading team got moving and pulled round; they went the wrong side of the lantern.

Swearing drivers whipped the horses in a hopeless attempt to drag the wagon out. The sergeant with the lantern added his loud cursing to the chorus. A salvo of H.E. dashed overhead. So the Boche was going to cover the battery again; the next salvo would in the ordinary course of Boche gunnery drop back into the middle of this block of transport.

"Silence! Unhook that team and leave the wagon there to-night." Phizz gave a hand himself, and the team was soon clear. "Walk march away. Halt in Vermelles, and no trotting!" He guided the remaining teams round himself. The last team was pulling round, with Phizz very anxiously keyed up for the arrival of the next salvo, which was just about due. "Steady there!" he called, as the centre driver whipped at his horse. The horse stumbled and fell dead. Caught in the flank by a stray from the first close burst of shrapnel, it had struggled on without a sign till at last it was finished.

Now a dead horse can be dropped out of a team in military equipment without interference with the rest, but in six months of perfectly peaceful war the driver had forgotten how. He stood there looking at it as it lay a darker patch in the black mud. And Phizz too waited. It was too late now to get clear: would the next salvo smash into them, or not? And this was his own section's best team, all black, and no horse to replace the one already dead. His own personal risk never struck his imagination, not because he deliberately shelved it, but simply because he had got used to shelling in his days at O.P. But then he had been on his own, as it were, with no responsibility for others to multiply anxiety, until at this first experience of it he felt the burden intolerable, standing helpless in the rain and the mud and the inky blackness, with disordered wagon-teams, gunners spread across the position stumbling about with ammunition, and the certainty in his mind that the next few seconds would see the pitiless burst of a German salvo pitching in the middle of them. Would those shells never come? - he seemed to have stuck there inactive for an eternity, though it was really but a few seconds. He began to free the dead horse himself, he dragged a trace out of the mud. His cold fingers could hardly manipulate the release. At last it was ready.

"Here, sergeant, give a hand on the wheels! Now, drive on."

Sergeant Piggott heaved and tugged at one wheel of the limber, Phizz at the other. The wheels skidded round in the mud as they strained on the spokes. The weakened, frightened team pulled, and jibbed. The off-leader, backing away from an injudicious lash, slipped in an old trench. She splashed and strained in an agony of fear and scrambled out. Heaving the limber, almost by sheer lifting Phizz and the sergeant got it moving. The wheelers jerked forward, the team took the strain, the wagon lurched forward, and they were away at a fast walk. The expected salvo never came. The Hun had finished.

Phizz had never felt such extraordinary relief before. As he stood there his own risk remained nearly exactly what it had been, but to have got away these men and horses, for whom he was responsible, made the whole incident appear to be over. Sergeant Piggott brought the lantern along to light the way back to the gun position. But suddenly he stopped.

"I think I have been hit, sir!"

"Where, Piggott?" Phizz asked in amazement. By contrast with the relief of his mind, the idea that his sergeant was wounded came as a real shock.

He looked and saw Piggott's hand smeared red and his right side dripping with a slow trickle of blood. "Good Heavens, Piggott, I'm sorry to see that. Lean on me and I'll help you in, and then get Mr. Gurney to look after you. He will have arrived back from O.P. by now." Gurney had been a medical student before the war.

"I can still walk, sir," the sergeant said, slowly putting his weight on the right leg; "only I think I'm getting a bit faint, sir."

"Then sit down here, and I'll call some men to carry you in. Now wait, don't try to get in yourself; that is the very worst thing possible."

Phizz left the light with Piggott and ran across to send a bearer party to bring him in. This was the first casualty on the gun position, and several of the gunners ran over to the light to help the sergeant.

Phizz went as quickly as he could to the mess for Gurney.

"You're late for dinner, Phizz," said the Major as he came in; then as he caught sight of his soaked and mud-stained clothes he went on, "What on earth has happened? Have you fallen in the mud?"

"No, Major, we had trouble with the transport. Didn't you hear the shelling?"

"Oh, I thought I heard something, but it sounded as if it were all short, and you weren't even retaliating."

"Well, they have killed George, out of my black team, and wounded Piggott: pretty badly, I should say. I came over at once to get Gurney to come and see to it."

Gurney, who had changed into slippers after he got back from O.P., did not stop to put boots on. He and the Major both followed Phizz along the muddy track to the B sub. gun pit. However, they were too late - for the dénouement of the comic opera episode in which Phizz had unwittingly assisted was already accomplished. Whether the hen in Piggott's pocket had possibly been hit by shrapnel in that burst which had killed "George," or (as is much more likely) whether she had merely been torn and squashed to death as he heaved on the wheel of the ammunition wagon, was never solved. But the blood on his hand and his own imagination had really made him feel faint, and the stain on his clothes had done the rest.

That is the detailed history of how C/XYZ were first engaged by the Hun.

And though it should sound more like a stage farce than real war, yet it is not unlikely that·to it may be ascribed much of that subsequent courage and endurance which made the battery one to be proud of. The "needle" is a nasty thing, and not easy to cure, but it would indeed be a virulent attack of it that could survive such a comic opera introduction to bombardment as it was the good luck of C/XYZ to have.

CHAPTER IV

A night patrol.

Gunner liaison officer in an infantry battalion -
concern over an earth mound being built by the Germans -
Thurston volunteers to join a night patrol to investigate.

THE Vimy ridge rises up from the valley of the Souchez river
with much the same outline and general shape as a sleeping cow. Its
head is held up to the south, and its great haunches sweep round
from the north end to spread under the main ridge in foot-hills
pointing towards Souchez village. A flat swamp lies between the
belly of the ridge and the village, about half a mile across. Up the
steep flanks of the beast there used to run a deep and angular trench
making its way towards the saddle, across which in more smiling
times the hill road to Givenchy had wound its way; but about

half-way up the slope this trench suddenly dwindled away into a battered ditch as it lost itself under the wire of No Man's Land, in the shapeless waste of water-logged shell-craters which marked the end of the German advance in February, 1916.

The warm morning sun of a perfect spring day was drying up the ragged wounds of this shattered hillside. Rank patches of green grass offset by big yellow cowslips had already overgrown the more sheltered patches, and on one such rough carpet lay Phizz, his head up against one of the steep terraces which outline the cultivated hills of Northern France. A neglected magazine by his side betrayed the absence of purpose with which he lay there, risking all the evils which the doctors threaten to those who lie on damp earth. Below him lay Souchez and the swampy river valley. Now there is a critical point in the work of destruction beyond which each further smashing explosion only reduces a monument of tortured ruin into a flatter barrenness. Poor old Ypres, for instance, passed this point on the day when the echoing of an enemy shell shook down the last tottering wall of St. Martin's tower. Montauban and Bazentin, Messines and Zonnebeke, had passed it before the advancing barrage lifted over them in front of our attacking infantry. The warm red brick of Albert or Bailleul could never reach it as they crumbled away now under the enemy guns, now under our own. But Souchez lay there in front of Phizz, the acme of human desolation, utterly crashed into abominable rottenness, yet still thrusting up from the rank and swollen marsh the wretched stumps which told of the wasted industry of men, the lost happiness of women. The tiny cemetery, for the possession of which hundreds of men had been hurled into death, lay unmarked by the least relic of stone or marble only the unalleviated foulness of stagnant waterlogged shell hole bitten into the cankered lips of another and another and another; and yet the rusted iron gate still stood up crazily, without supporting posts, waiting half-opened. Of the church the only relic was the strong bell-beam, leaning silently against the one remaining pillar of the entrance gate. The heaped ruins of the houses of the village lay among stripped and broken tree trunks. Two trees only still had branches, which creaked black and forbidding over the very heart of this abomination, where once had been the Chateau Carieul. A huge iron vat from the sugar refinery grinned through its gaping lid at the end of the village, though around it was nothing but flattened wreckage. From behind it, crawled a narrow wooden track winding in and out among the craters of the marsh, broken here and there, and patched up everywhere, until it came out of the plain into the concealment of the foothills and led straight up to the ridge for its last hundred yards. By day it was an impossible path, with death shadowing each inch of its way across the marsh: by night it was "unhealthy." Away on the right the gaunt grey ruin of the church tower of Ablain St. Nazaire shone in the sun, pointing up its strikingly bizarre finger in mockery. And in the background of this picture of Battle's aftermath lay a distant fringe of sprouting woods, just flecked with the light green of early leaves, budding into new life and smiling towards the desolate ridge with their cheery lesson of the kindliness of Nature.

However, Phizz was not only not impressed, but had not the slightest interest in it: he was dreaming of his expected leave and the week of cleanliness and comfort which it meant: and of one whom he would meet once more to crown the delight of it all. April dreams are not of war even in the middle of it. Undisturbed in his pleasant anticipation, he heard a long-range whizz-bang whistle over the ridge and spit out a vicious rain of bullets over the 'duckboards.' Then another followed, and Phizz heard a call from the trench some twenty yards below him.

"Gunner! Gunner!" It was the sharp voice of the little colonel of the battalion to which Phizz was attached. Each battalion had an artillery subaltern attached to it as a means of liaison between the gunners and the men they were supporting. These officers took turns of duty of about four days or a week at a time, and

Phizz had been unlucky enough to get his present tour with a very irascible battalion commander, who had, moreover, just previously suffered from the attachment of a rather annoying and incapable gunner. Phizz's dream was thoroughly burst now, but he waited some minutes before slipping down the hillside and into the deep trench. He was walking on past his own dugout entrance as a telephonist thrust his head up from it.

"Mr. Thurston, I was just coming out to find you. The infantry colonel wants to see you."

"Right, thanks! I'm going along to him now."

A few yards beyond the next corner was a timbered dugout entrance at the bottom of the trench, with a sentry standing opposite beside a gas-alarm gong. Phizz climbed backwards down the steps, which ended about ten feet down in a little deal-panelled room about six feet by eight. Across one end were two sleeping bunks, the upper of which was tilted back so that the bottom one could be used as a bench. A fixed wooden table took up the middle of the room, and a wooden form on two sides filled up all the rest of the space. At first the change from the open sunlight prevented Phizz from seeing anything in the dugout, but the colonel, invisible to him as yet, snapped out, "Well, have you done anything?"

"With regard to what?" asked Phizz quietly.

"The shelling, of course; haven't you seen it?"

"I saw four shrapnel bursts on the duckboards, but that is all."

"That is all! and quite enough too. Aren't you going to retaliate?"

"Well, sir, he isn't doing any harm at all, for there is nobody there; and if he were, retaliation would probably only annoy him into keeping on with it.

The Major dislikes retaliation unless we can give the Boche as good as we get."

"And what about us, the 'P.B. Infantry'? We have our relief on to-night, and do you want to let the Hun shell us to hell without doing a thing? All you gunners are the same!"

If you want retaliation, sir, you can have the exact amount you choose to ask for every time they fire on the duckboards."

"What is the use of retaliating if you can't do any good with your gun?"

Phizz smiled under cover of the general dinginess of the dugout at this change of front. "I heard from our officer at O.P. half an hour ago, sir, that he had spotted the battery which was doing this shooting, and tried to get the Heavies to engage it. Also he is shooting at it himself now, I think."

The Colonel grunted, and climbed out of the dugout, followed by Phizz. The soft report of an 18-pounder firing at long range could be heard intermittently. The shelling of the duckboards had stopped.

"Why aren't the Heavies firing too?" the Colonel growled.

Phizz suggested some possible reasons without including the probable one that the counter-battery group might prefer to deal with the enemy battery at their own time rather than his. But he was interrupted by one of his telephonists.

"Brigade Headquarters to speak to you on the phone sir."

Phizz excused himself and went to his own dugout. Its name literally described it completely, for it simply was a hole dug out from the trench side and roughly propped up with odd pieces of timber. Two riskylooking bunks had been fixed up with wire netting, and on the upper one were Phizz's blankets; below, the signaller off duty was sleeping, undisturbed by the two beady-eyed little mice who scampered over him to the far corner of the bed as Phizz pushed his way inside. In the doorway was a little brazier with a steak grilling pleasantly over it. Behind was an upturned ammunition box with the 'phone close at hand. Phizz took it up and spoke.

"Hallo, is that the Adjutant?"

"One moment, sir," the signaller holding the line at the other end answered him. Then the Adjutant's voice came on: "Hallo, Thurston."

"Morning, Adj."

"I say, Phizz, the Colonel wanted to come down to Battalion Headquarters this morning, but the infantry Brigadier has told him you can't be reached by day. You got down there in daylight, didn't you?"

"Yes," Phizz replied, "but it is rather round-about and a lot of it though under cover is nowhere near a trench. Infantry don't seem to use it at all, I don't know why."

"What is the way you mean?"

"Oh, round by Carency, and down Ersatz, which is one of the trenches in that sector, as far as the bottom of the ridge; then along either of the bottom terraces you are completely covered as far as here if you keep close up."

The Adjutant went off the line for a moment, then called again: "Hallo, Phizz; we are going to ride over to Carency, and then walk. Will you meet us at the top of Ersatz, and act as guide?"

"Right-ho; goodbye." Phizz went out to tell the infantry Colonel that his C.O. was corning down; the answer was another growl.

"I don't believe you are out of sight going across from here. You will be getting yourselves killed, which is your own pigeon; but in addition, you will be giving my headquarters away."

"I am sure, sir, that it is only in view from near Calonne, and that is too far to matter," Phizz answered.

Soon afterwards he set off to meet his C.O. and the Adjutant, and returned with them nearly two hours later. Meanwhile a message had already reached the battalion with the same information that the C.O. was bringing to Phizz. Near the top of the ridge there had been slowly growing an irregular pile of brown earth which had been nicknamed the "Pimple." It was in a most advantageous position for observation, so much so that for miles around it had become one of the most striking landmarks on the sky-line. Air photographs showed it moreover as a strong point well organised for defence. The General had decided that it must be destroyed, and all the heavy batteries in the area would concentrate on it at three o'clock that afternoon, while field batteries harassed the remainder of the ridge so as to keep down counter-observation and generally annoy the Boche.

The infantry Colonel was still swearing hard when the party of gunners arrived at his headquarter dugout. He just wished the C.O. good morning, then flowed on with his indiscriminate tide of vituperation. "What about my relief to-night? They will stir up the Hun with this shoot until he makes the duckboards absolutely impassable. I might lose half my battalion, getting out. The General has kept us in too long already, in these filthy trenches; and what with trench feet and rheumatism, my strength is low enough now, and he wants to make me lose the rest." He asked what earthly reason there could be for arranging the bombardment that day of all others.

"There is a twelve-inch howitzer taking part, which has to pack up and go down south to-morrow, so it could not be put off," explained the artillery commander; "but I believe your relief is put off until after one a.m., so as to give you just time to get out and yet be late enough to miss any ordinary strafe on the duckboards."

The Colonel's wrath boiled away after a few more violent moments, and the whole party crowded into the tiny dugout for lunch - the infantry Colonel, his second in command and adjutant, and the three gunners. It was quite a good meal, and whisky in enamel mugs with chlorinated water was not enough to spoil the zest of a trench appetite; afterwards a box of fairly well-kept cigars was passed round, to be enjoyed with some light port. The host toned down his bitterness into a general grouse about the sector he was holding. The front line consisted of three isolated 'grouse-butts,' manned each by a platoon: and of these only the right hand one could be approached by day - along the trench they were then in. The conditions were so bad that the men could not be kept in for more than 24 hours at a time. The reserve company was some miles away, near Ablain, and was completely useless by day since the duckboards were impassable. His supporting and relief companies were crowded together in a chalk quarry further along the hill; true, the dugouts tunnelled from the quarry into the hillside were safe enough, but they were inadequate and unventilated, and meant sardine-like packing; while accurate enemy whizz-banging made the open quarry itself an absolute death-trap. The centre grouse-butt was open to enfilade fire from the north, and while any attempt to make the post stronger was promptly punished, it was still impossible to get wounded away until dark. Yet our hold on these grouse-butts was absolutely essential for the safety of the Vimy ridge; (and, if this anticipation may be pardoned, when the Boche made his attempt two months later to push us off the ridge altogether, backed by the most dramatic concentration of artillery on a very narrow front that perhaps ever occurred throughout the War, these grouse-butts held up the flank and did not give. They remained in our hands but little changed when in the following year they were the pivot for that advance of the "Byng Boys," which was one of the critical steps to final victory).

In view of the coming heavy bombardment, the 'right picquet' would have to be withdrawn from their grouse-butt, which was within a hundred yards or so of the Pimple, and so within the danger zone from our own fire. The Colonel walked up there with Phizz and his C.O., stopping for a few minutes at his right Company headquarters a few yards further up the trench. The trench got shallower and narrower as it climbed the hill; in the last straight bit were several overhead barriers of sandbagging, to stop the view from the Pimple above down into the exposed trench. At the top it ended in a sandbag block, while the uncared-for ditch which had once been its continuation dwindled away into No Man's Land. On the right hand side was a small post settled in a black earth trench without sandbagging or revetment. On the left a very narrow ditch with a sandbag parapet was filled

44

with muddy figures in khaki. In front and behind the parapet were great shell-holes full of stagnant green water, which would not soak away. A constant trickle of foul water washed down the splashing bottom of the trench, and any attempt at working had so far yielded little better than a deluge of pent-up water which would wash away the sandbagging, and often much of the trench as well. The officers pushed past the men in the grouse-butt, squeezing into the muddy wall to get by; they crawled under low overhead shelters of corrugated iron and scrappy sandbagging, the whole dripping and oozing heavily, though no rain had fallen for some days. At last they came to another such shelter, but lower and blocked up at the far end; it was packed with waterproof sheets and empty sandbags, and comparatively was snug and warm. A signaller sat by a small telephone lying half-overturned among the sandbags. At the other end was the officer in charge, wrapped in a trench coat with his feet inside sandbags: though the day was quite warm, the inactivity and dirt and mud demanded special means of keeping up circulation and warmth. He began to crawl out of the shelter, but the Colonel stopped him and asked after his men, told him of the coming withdrawal, and added that the company commander would soon be up to arrange it. So they crawled back again; Phizz glancing cautiously out past this shelter saw the trench continuing beyond it as a battered but just recognisable ditch of mud and pent-up water, with the sandbags of the centre picquet just recognisable some two hundred yards away. Before they started back down the communication trench, the C.O. asked Phizz if he would be able to watch the shooting at the Pimple from any point near there as a check on the distant observation and on short-shooting. Phizz, feeling grimly that this was the only possible place, and that if there were any short-shooting his interest in stopping it would be considerably greater than his chance of getting it stopped, answered that he could find a place; and the party returned.

"Would you like to go along to the Quarry?" the Colonel asked the visiting gunners; but the C.O. wished to be back in time for the opening of the bombardment, and for this it was quite time he left. Phizz now got one of his signallers to help him with laying a telephone line up 'Holloway' - the communication trench; they were hampered by the withdrawn infantry coming down it to the dugouts below, but at last it was finished up to the top of the trench, and Phizz connected up a 'phone, tested the line, and then sent his man back to the dugout. For some time he was looking through a periscope at the German lines, clearly visible as a strong parapet on the sky-line of the ridge. The gruff voice of the Colonel sounded behind him.

"You haven't got your shrapnel helmet on I expected your own C.O. to curse you for being such a damned fool, but he didn't."

Phizz remembered that, for the first time, he had seen his C.O. uncomfortably balancing on his head the inverted iron porringer which had recently been supplied to the infantry and to only the officers among the gunners.

"Well, I'm sorry, sir, I—er—forgot mine. You see, none are supplied for the telephonists and I didn't—er— notice," he stammered out his untruthful excuse; "besides, they are so heavy and hard, and I'm sure they couldn't stop a bullet."

"How in thunder does that excuse you from the order that they have to be worn. I won't have it disobeyed in my trenches at any rate. Run down and get my batman to give you the spare one in my dugout which didn't fit me."

Phizz, very much annoyed if the truth be told, walked back as quickly as he could; but almost before he had returned, the lumbering rush of heavy howitzer shells had begun with a chorus of yapping field guns shooting all along the ridge. As each heavy round thudded into the soft ground the earth pulsed with a deep heart-straining throb. Phizz, in the picquet alone and uncomfortable, watched the Pimple as each tremor corresponded with a shower of great clods of earth tossed straight up into the air to about forty feet. But the shooting was nearly all "safe" going rather beyond the target so that the inevitable short rounds might not drop in our own lines. Phizz buzzed on his 'phone and sent a message through to that effect, though this did not prevent his feeling distinctly hopeful on his own account that the haughty Heavies would disdain the field gunner's correction and go on shooting safe. However, about half-way through, a very bad round dropped short below him somewhere to his right; he looked across at it, smiling momentarily to himself as a field gunner at the inefficiency of those incompetent slackers the Garrison Artillery, when he fell into the bottom of the trench with a dazed impression of a shattering clang in his ears. He was looking round in half angry surprise to discover what had happened, when his eye caught the glint of a clean bright sliver of steel, its rough edge sticking up from the mud in the trench. He picked it up, but dropped it again quickly as it burned his fingers. Then from behind him he pulled out of the mud his 'tin hat' A wide dent in the brim with the green paint scratched off told of the narrow escape he had had, and he felt more than a bit sheepish as he realised what he owed to the Colonel's brusque order, so ill-humouredly obeyed. He wiped the mud off the helmet, put it on carefully, and moved across to another part of the butt where the deeper wall gave him additional protection from the rear. But for the remainder of the shoot nothing happened at all; no very pronounced difference in the Pimple could be seen, and no more rounds dropped short. When it was all over he went back to tell the infantry that the picquet was all clear. The enemy had fired barely a round in retaliation; and without mentioning his lucky escape he went down the dugout to tea.

"Hallo, Gunner," the second-in-command greeted him, "is there anything of the Pimple left?"

Phizz laughed. "I don't think you'll fail to recognise it when you see it."

"It was the feeblest thing in the way of bombardments I've ever heard," the other rejoined; he had passed .the afternoon dozing on his bunk in the dugout, but that did not interfere with his criticising the operation.

The adjutant chipped in: "Feeble wasn't the word for it. I don't believe .there were ever two rounds in the air together. Half the time I was wondering if it had been cancelled or not."

"I dare say the jolly old Huns in the Pimple had less doubt about it. You know it's an amazing thing how your impression differs according to whether shells are going over you or coming at you. Now how many rounds do you think were fired altogether?"

The adjutant thought a moment."Oh, a hundred and twenty about, I should say."

"Yes, and actually there were over eight hundred according to the artillery programme."

"Then there shouldn't be anything left of the dashed place if you gunners are worth your salt!" Phizz knew quite well that most of the firing had been at too long a range, and that the smashing up of the Pimple had not actually been accomplished, but he felt no call to disillusion the infantryman as to the efficiency of the Artillery, even though they were speaking of the rival branch of the gunners for whom he had then a healthy contempt. He tried to lead the conversation gently round.

"The Boche must have been pretty anxious, to hold his retaliation back as he has done."

"Well, I thought he was going to begin down here just after half-past three," replied the second-in command.

Phizz, realising the bad short which he had such reason to remember, decided that the conversation might perhaps soon need another turn. But the Colonel came down and caused the necessary diversion. He held in his hand a pink message slip; as he sat down he pushed it across to his second-incommand with a short comment as lurid as the sheet itself.

"Brigade say we must send out a reconnoitring patrol to see what has happened to this —— Pimple; and that on relief night! Curse these blank gunners and their d——d bombardments! Why can't they patrol themselves if they can't see if they have hit the thing or not? Get hold of Williams after tea and tell him to detail Warren and what men he wants ; but warn them against getting into a scrap. There must be no fighting at all, and if the Boche patrols are out they must come back." He glared at the empty teapot, and the Adjutant called up the steps for more tea. The waiter came down with a fresh pot and another pink form in his hand. The Adjutant glanced at it while the Colonel went on with his tea.

"Good Lord, sir," he burst out, "the Boche has retaliated into the Quarry and caught the Doctor there as well as five men and his corporal too. What can we do? Shall I ask right battalion to send their M.O. across?"

"No, of course not: he couldn't get across here even if you did."

"He might come the same way that I brought Colonel Wormald this morning, sir," Phizz interrupted, "I would go, and bring him across."

"This is my business," the Colonel snapped. "I have forbidden anyone to cross that exposed area, and you will bear that in mind yourself for the future, please."

"Really, sir, you are not exposed if you go the right way about it," Phizz began, but stopped as the Adjutant answered the buzzing of the little telephone on his bed.

"This is worse, sir," the Adjutant broke in.·

"Centre Picquet are on the 'phone to say that one shrapnel burst has enfiladed the post, and wounded eleven men: some will be pretty serious by the time it is dark enough to get them out."

"Say that I will do what I can for them. Gunner, retaliation at once!"

Phizz, who was already on the stairs, ran along to his dugout. He 'phoned up the battery, asking for sharp retaliation. Then he was put through to Gurney at O.P., and speaking with some difficulty on account of the barking of the retaliation rounds as they shot over, he asked him to keep a specially close look-out for a battery enfilading the centre picquet from a village two miles further north, and to swamp it quickly if it opened.

As he left his dugout to return and report to the Colonel, the Adjutant met him. "The Colonel has changed his mind and wants you to go over to right battalion with a runner and guide the M.O. back to the Quarry. He has fixed it up on the 'phone. The runner is ready here."

Phizz went off at once, and soon after had brought the Doctor to the Quarry. It was a very ordinary little chalk pit in the side of the hill, littered with empty petrol tins, rubber boots, and picks and shovels. Two or three low galleries with timber supports could be seen leading into the chalk walls, with the glow of candle-light on the dense "fugg" inside; but the uninteresting little galleries gave no idea of the number of human rabbits whose burrow they were. The orderly led the doctor crouching into the main gallery, where the wounded, roughly bandaged up, were lying on the floor. Phizz wandered off to the top of the quarry as far as the end of the little trench which led out of it. He raised his head to peep across to the isolated picquet where the other wounded were waiting. Over a broken morass strewn with the wreckage of old revetment and entanglements, he saw in a slight hollow an irregular line of mud-soaked sandbags. A few green helmets moved occasionally under the parapet. On the right, where the ground behind the grouse-butt was fairly flat, were two formless heaps covered with a loose waterproof sheet which glistened with a chill gleam through the liquid mud that had splashed it. A boot protruded and a dirty shrapnel helmet weighted down the windward corner of the sheet.

Phizz was not yet hardened to taking no notice of such things. He turned and tried to drive out more morbid thoughts by an imaginative sympathy with the remaining wounded, lying in the bottom of the post, exposed to such another burst as had cut them down, bleeding, faint, cold. An echoing crack - a singing in his right ear and the splashes of mud on his face effectively stopped his imagination. He crouched in the trench wondering from what direction the sniper had shot at his exposed head. Another vicious crack: and the ping of a bullet crashing through the too flimsy block of fascines which ended the trench told that the sniper was not giving up hope. Phizz ran for a bend in the little trench which protected him; and there he had the lunatic inspiration to wave his handkerchief over the top so that the Boche might not have the satisfaction of thinking he had scored; then he walked back to the quarry. There was a loud bang behind him, out of which came the vicious whistling ping of a rain of shrapnel bullets, and it checked him on the edge of the quarry. As he deserved, he had stirred up the observer of an enemy battery to try his hand in the game. Another bang, and a more angry whistling shut him inside a hail of splashing lead: on every yard of ground around him had fallen some of the three hundred bullets blown out of the shell, and by that chance which favours the drunken and the fool, he was unhurt in the middle of it. He laughed aloud as he jumped lightly down into the quarry and slipped into the shelter of its near side. His heart was beating high, he was exhilarated by the excitement of ·such narrow escapes, and an extraordinary consciousness of protection or luck or fatalism gave him a magnificent confidence. He walked back to battalion headquarters swinging his thick walking stick and whistling the last thing of Teddie Gerard's he had heard on the gramophone.

"Well, Gunner," the Adjutant greeted him, meeting him in the trench, what are you so sad about?

"Sad? Au contraire, I was just beginning to think the war would end before Christmas."

"I should damned well hope so, but that shouldn't make you mope around whistling the Dead March."

"My dear fellow, that was one of the latest and best things in rag-time. Have you no soul for music?

"Sorry," the other grinned; "try sticking up a programme card next time so that we don't waste our sympathy. But if you are so cheerful as all that, you might try to soothe the 'old man.' The whisky won't last out the night, and that on top of the other things has about broken the patient camel's back. He's abso. unbearable now, and I'm just strolling down the trench to be out of his way. Come along as far as the Quarry."

"Well, I was just going to see the Colonel to ask him to let me go out with your patrol to-night," Phizz answered.

"Good Lord, what a thing to want to do! Have you ever been out on night patrol before?"

Phizz said he had not.

"Then take my advice," the other went on, "and don't. It is infernally unpleasant and dirty, it's dangerous without being exciting, and to be quite honest about it, I don't see that this patrol can do the least bit of good."

"Oh I think that too; but I would like just to see for myself what No Man's Land is like at night."

"Right-ho; in any case the Old Man won't let you, but tackle him if you like. Personally I'm a peaceable sort of cove, and the longer I can keep this headquarter job, the better I'm pleased: he is a bit of a trial at times though, you may have noticed. I shall see you at dinner," he added over his shoulder as he strolled on.

Phizz went along to the battalion commander's private dugout. At the bottom of the steps was a blanket-curtain. "Are you there, sir?" Phizz called through it.

"What do you want?" snapped the Colonel.

Phizz made his way inside and found him sitting at a small box table with a paper map on it, lit by two candles stuck on cigarette tin lids. An empty enamel mug had been pushed across to the other side.

"May I go out with the patrol to the Pimple to-night, sir?" Phizz went straight to the point.

"Leave your own job here and go fooling around for your own amusement? Is that what your brigade send you here for?"

"If anything were wanted, sir, my telephonists could ring up for it as well as I could; and you said this afternoon that the gunners ought to do their own reconnaissance. I thought you would like to have one of your own men relieved."

"And have a clumsy fool of a gunner drawing fire on the others and getting the lot scuppered! You've done enough damage to-day with this pea-shooting bombardment of yours already."

"Very good, sir. I didn't mention it before perhaps, but I have been all over this bit of No Man's Land by *daylight*, which none of your own officers have, I think," Phizz answered.

"What on earth do you mean, about going over it by daylight?" asked the Colonel.

"A month ago, when the Division first carne in, and your Brigade was in reserve, sir, I was here with the first of our battalions, just after relieving the French. It was not long after the German advance, and both sides were in conditions far worse even than these grouse-butts now. There was nothing for it but live and let live. It wasn't fraternising exactly, but they used to let us walk about within reason, and of course we let them too. I went across one morning just after two Boches had come over to what is now the centre picquet; and I tried to practise my German on a Boche sentry in the line where the Pimple now is. He had on one of the English cyclist's capes, I remember, and I couldn't recollect the German for 'cyclist,' let alone for 'cape,' to ask him where he got it. In any case it was no good: they apparently had orders not to talk, and I had to come back as wise as I went. In the same way they used to fire three 'minnies' each afternoon, but they always pitched them where they would do no harm, and blew a whistle beforehand. I think it is our fault things have changed, for the Boche seems to have been only anxious to be left in peace to work on the Pimple."

"Hmmm, well, I haven't time to listen to yarns now," the Colonel interrupted Phizz: "Go and tell Captain Williams I want him; he will be in the Company dugout," the Colonel called after him.

Phizz delivered the message on his way up the trench, then went on as far as the Right Picquet. The men were at arms for the evening stand-to, some swaying from one foot to the other to help circulation, others leaning quietly against the muddy wall. Their packs, neatly fixed up for marching away on relief, were propped up in front of them. Two were quarrelling hoarsely about a missing oil-bottle; they caught sight of Phizz, and recognising him as an officer, shut down. Phizz used the. last minutes of waning daylight in looking through his periscope at the lie of the ground between him and the Pimple, thinking of the route he would have chosen. It looked comparatively smooth after the first yards of deep shell-hole pools and scattered entanglement, but he knew how deceptively the foreshortened view hid a torn morass, which even by day looked practically impassable.

"Good evening. Did you hit it this afternoon?" Phizz turned without moving his periscope; a subaltern who had come along the grouse-butt was speaking.

"Oh, I think the trenches there have been pretty well smashed up, but the Pimple itself looks pretty solid still. Have you seen it?"

"No; may I?" He looked through the periscope, but, unused to the magnification of the artillery pattern, he recognised very little. "Yes, it is very interesting," he murmured politely as he handed it back to Phizz; "I am going out there to-night to see what has really happened."

Phizz reflected superciliously on the infantryman's confidence in his night reconnaissance, as against what the artillery O.P.'s could see by day. But the other went on: "I wonder what the Pimple really is?"

"Well, no one seems very sure about it," Phizz answered. "The air photographs all show it as a sort of strong point, but Intelligence persist in calling it an O.P. I am sure there are no loopholes to be seen there by day, and if anybody does use it as an O.P., he must be pretty plucky. Then you fellows have reported it as a machine-gun nest. Personally I think the mound is only an accident, from the digging of the trenches around it or dugouts perhaps; and the place is really an organised strong point only - and a very good place for one, too!"

The two officers were joined by a third, coming up the communication trench.

"All O.K., Warren?"

"Yes, thanks, Skipper. Here is the Gunner, having a look at the damage he did this afternoon."

"Oh, are you the gunner who wants to go out on this patrol to-night? I am Williams, you know."

"Good evening. I did ask your Colonel, but there was nothing doing," Phizz answered.

"You're a bigger fool than I'd have guessed you to be," said the other abruptly; "but the Colonel told me Warren could take you if he likes. He leaves it to him."

Warren broke in heartily: "Come by all means if you want to. There are a few tips I shall have to give you, but you will be all right. I shall go over at ten, so stay to dinner with us, won't you?"

Phizz accepted, and stayed chatting for some minutes in the growing darkness. Then the order "Stand down" was passed along. There was a shuffling off of equipment, an unfixing of bayonets: and the men who were not left on sentry duty moved about the trench a little to ease their stiffness before settling down in the trench, or squeezing in under the little stretches of crazy overhead cover. Warren handed over with a nod to another officer who had come up, and Williams and Phizz went down Holloway to the Company dugout. Going down they passed a couple of men carrying up a steaming dixey of tea which left behind it the pleasantly stimulating smell of an admixture of rum.

"You look after your fellows pretty well," Phizz commented.

"We have to, Williams answered, or we soon wouldn't have a man left. Sometimes it beats me how they stand at all. Their feet for instance - after thirty hours up to the knees in mud, some of them without gum-boots, and all of them swollen with cold, they will have to march out to Aix, halt there for breakfast, then on for another five miles to Coupigny: that after all this time without sleep, too! If only we could have one scrap and be done with it! But we go on losing men in this deadly dull game, and never get an inch further. Yet they carry on all the same, reinforcements nearly as well as the old hands who haven't had the luck to get a 'Blighty one' yet. If you went up there now, you would find them sharing their ration of jam out of the tin and eating biscuits and great slabs of cheese, with or without the jam; and talking about their missus, or their old towns, or how to win the war, just as you might do comfortably settled in an armchair after dinner at your club. There is hardly ever the bitterness in it, though, that you get from those bloated old bores at home who complain of everything from the waiter to old man Asquith. Well, here we are," he wound up as they reached the dugout.

This dugout was simply a narrow sloping shaft cut into the hillside for about fifty feet; at the far end it had been scooped out to a rather increased width, and here Williams lit three or four candles. A somewhat rickety and roughly carpentered table was pushed against the side of the wall, with some upturned ammunition boxes serving as stools at the near end and in the very narrow space left along the opposite side. Beyond this a stretcher on the floor and a loose waterproof sheet and some loose sandbags on the ground alongside, were two of the beds of this compact little bed-sitting-room. A third was at present bundled out of the way, under the table. The roof was lined with an old French waterproof sheet, pegged in with cartridges; this was to stop the earth shaking down on the table, but a scampering of mice as the candles were lit threw down a shower of grit on Phizz, who being uninitiated was stooping just below the edge of it. The scraping of a rat over the wood framing of the shaft bespoke the parting of another self-invited guest. A batman who had waited for them came down and spread a newspaper sheet over the table and laid knives and forks and plates and mugs, with a half-loaf of ration bread face down on the table, and salt and pepper screwed up in paper. From the end of his stretcher-bed Williams produced some bottles: one a Martini, another old whisky bottle with Rum scrawled over the label, another really containing whisky, and a fourth with the blue label of Expeditionary Force Canteen port.

"Cocktail, Gunner?" he asked.

"Thanks very much. But, I say, you do yourselves well on the 'poison,' don't you?"

"Oh, well enough," Williams answered; "it's the only way, you know, when you are in the line. The funny thing is, too, I missed half the fun at Cambridge by being T.T. Even now I go very easy when we are out of the line, but we just take enough here to keep the blood going round, don't you know."

Some Oxo soup was brought into the dugout in a jug and poured out on flat enamel plates. Except for the speed with which it cooled, it was excellent. Then came a tin of sardines; butter was on the table in a dumpy round ration tin. Warren began a discussion on the position which the sardines should have had in the menu; whether hors d'œuvres or savoury, or as they had come, "en poisson." With a fine impartiality he decided that they might be anything other than fish, but as they had come in the wrong place he would make the best of it; and he wolfed a double share.

"I say, Warren," began Williams as he stretched over for the butter tin, "who is the blighter who leaves the jam from his knife on the butter? How often must I din it into the heads of you young novices that the way to take more butter with a jammy knife is to attack with the side of your knife, and scoop, not cut the butter out - comme ca, merci bien. Do you appreciate my scholarly French, Gunner?" he turned to Phizz.

"Oui, Oui, comment!" Phizz grinned.

"Right you are, now you can have some vin des tranchées as your prize. Help yourself to the whisky; the water is in the petrol can just by your side."

Phizz filled up his mug and passed the can round to Warren. His whisky was subtly perfumed with a suspicion of petrol, and the taste was slightly modified by a too liberal sterilisation with chloride of lime; but even so, it might have been worse - there might not have been any whisky!

The meat course turned out by Williams' cook was a piping hot dish of bully-beef rissoles, garnished with potatoes and dried carrots. It was delayed a little, while the soup plates were washed and wiped with a sandbag, to reappear slightly moist (for a sandbag is not an ideal dish-wiper) but also slightly warm. Phizz complimented his hosts on the excellence of their cook.

"He is not so bad," Williams agreed deprecatingly; "he is an improvement on the one we had before; that was the batman who is waiting on us to-night. He used to be in the kitchen of the R.A.C., but he was quite hopeless without his electric stoves and yards of saucepans or whatever he used to have there. So we tried this fellow, who started life as a 'busconductor." The discussion of the cook's merits was stopped by the waiter coming in again with the sweet.

"Here we are again!" Warren sang out. "Try our world-renowned Plug Street fritters, then die. Are you brave enough to risk it?" he asked Phizz.

"They look quite tempting enough," said Phizz.

He took one of the fritters, a concoction of toasted biscuit, jam and condensed milk, which belied the unkind welcome given them by the fastidious Warren. Phizz lived through his experiment and was even rash enough to take a second.

"Don't let me seem inhospitable," said Williams, "but the cook's real chef d'œuvre lies ahead of you, and if you pass it by he will never forgive you."

"I think I can rise to it even now," Phizz answered, "but you have done me uncommonly well. Compared to our simple meals in the battery, your battalion headquarters seemed to keep a blatantly luxurious table, but I think you beat them."

Williams laughed. "Listen to the Gunner's blarney, Warren, trying to persuade us that they don't live the bloated life of aristocrats back at Bruay or wherever they hide their damned guns!"

"Oh, drop in on us some time when you are out of the line, and see for yourself what a simple life we lead. Our mess is the old Mairie in Ablain; do you know it?"

"Well, thanks awfully, but when I'm out of the line I prefer not to tempt Providence by joy-riding into Ablain. But seriously, we might fix up a Christian meal some evening in Bruay, at the old 'Commerce' say."

Over the cook's final dish they arranged to do this. They were eating toasted cheese of the most priceless india-rubbery elasticity, holding it in their fingers. Williams uncorked the port.

"Will you have a glass of port?" he invited. "I'm afraid it will have to be in the mug you have been using; but we can rinse it out if you like. I think there is water enough for that, as we are going out to-night, and the others will bring their own supply in." He shook the petrol tin. "Oh yes, lots of it," he went on, but Phizz preferred his mug as it was after draining the whisky and water, to rinsing it in the unadulterated chloride of lime solution.

After the port, a pot of thick strong tea was brought, as strong as stewing could make it; and with condensed milk and rum it took the place of after-dinner coffee. Smoking a long loosely-rolled 'Panatella,' Williams apologised for the absence of real coffee and liqueurs, as 'he had been told there was a war on.' Then for some minutes they all sat silently and comfortably thinking.

"Oh, come along, we must do something: eat more or drink more, any old thing, or I shall start thinking about the War, and we have half an hour to go yet. Do you play cut-throat, Gunner?"

Warren reached for a limp pack of cards from behind his bedding. Phizz was quite keen on a game of bridge, and the three settled down to a short rubber. Williams with a quick run of undeserved luck just pulled it off in time.

"Never mind, Gunner: unlucky in cards, lucky in love!" Williams laughed as the others paid up. "Now what about this patrol stunt - are still keen?"

Phizz stretched himself comfortably. The lights and the warmth of the little dugout were very pleasant, but with artificial enthusiasm he assured them he was.

Williams pulled on his heavy trench coat and equipment. "It is my turn on duty now," he said; "I will come up with you. You have given instructions to your party, haven't you, Warren? The Adjutant has warned Centre Picquet and the right battalion that you will be out. What arms are you taking, Gunner?"

Phizz had overlooked this point. "I can run down and get my shooter if it will be any good: or had I better have just a couple of bombs?"

Williams thought a moment. "The fewer firearms the better on these stunts, I always think, unless you are thoroughly used to it. I will lend you my truncheon, and that should do you well enough. In any case, if there is trouble you have to keep out of it, so it doesn't matter so much. And now what about clothes? Of course a trench coat is no good; I always use one of these leather jerkins turned inside out, as the flannel lining doesn't glisten when it is wet."

Phizz put one on, and they went out. At first it was difficult to see in the dark trench, but gradually they got their night eyes. It was a clear crisp night, just not freezing. The palpitating glare of an occasional Very light threw a heavy irregular shadow of the parapet down the trench, and showed up the hillside in a dirty ghostly mauve wherein everything seemed to be revealed and yet not a detail could be clearly seen. The occasional rattle of a distant machine-gun and the sudden soft reflection in the sky of red gun-flashes beyond the ridge, gave a satisfying feeling of life on the dead silent world of shadows.

Warren spoke quietly. "When we go out, you stick close behind me. The others will be behind us in case we want help. The great thing is to be quiet, and whatever happens don't disturb the Hun, for if we should run up against any of them and there is a dust-up, probably all of us would be done in by machine-gunning from both sides, so it wouldn't pay anybody. Then one other thing: if a Very light goes up, whatever you are doing and however you are, keep absolutely still. If you do they will never spot you, and if you try to drop into cover they certainly see your movement and you are for it."

"Right-ho, I'll take care. How do you intend to work it?"

"Oh, just go up as close to their wire as we can get, and listen to what they are doing for half an hour or so. Do you notice, by the way, that they keep sending their lights up: not enough to show that they are 'windy' and expecting us, but enough to indicate that they probably have no patrols out themselves."

They were met at the top of Holloway by the officer left on duty; Williams took over from him after a low word or two. Warren was whispering a few last instructions to the sergeant. The uncanny stillness of the air hung like a pall over their hushed voices, but the clear rattle of transport on pavé roads showed how well all sounds were travelling through the night atmosphere.

"This is where we go over. Ready?" Warren turned to Phizz.

"Rather!"

"Right; now quietly!" Quickly his silhouette showed on the low parapet, and he was over.

Phizz just realised that he had a heart, and it was beating double time; then cautiously he too stepped up on the bomb box which Warren had used, and flattening himself hard on the parapet wormed his way over and flopped into the hollow on the other side. There was a slight pop as a stream of sparks shot into the sky from in front of them and ended in a dazzling floating light. Everything near

Phizz was as clearly lit up as in a searchlight beam: each strand of the sandbags he had just crossed was as visible as by daylight: only by a definite effort could he compel his reason to overcome the impression that the enemy sentries saw him as clearly as he could see his own limbs. The loud crack of a rifle almost broke his rigid self-control, but as he realised that it had been fired away to a flank he stood outside himself mentally and cursed himself for a windy fool. He watched the light fall on to the ground and gutter away there; half dazzled, he tried to make out the enemy line, and saw nothing but the vague and jerky shadow of the crest. He heard an answering rifle shot from our own lines without a qualm, almost disinterestedly. The light had died out now, and hearing a low whispered whistle from in front, he made out the vague outline of Warren just about to go on. At the same time the sergeant dropped over beside him. A quiet "All right, sir?" and then one of the men in the trench kicked an empty tin and upset it with a rattle. Up shot another Very light, and down it floated towards them. Phizz saw it dropping apparently straight on to him and almost lost his acquired calmness, when it dropped in the water of a shell-hole only a few yards in front and went out with a vicious splutter. Again he made out Warren's form moving lightly and quickly forward on all fours. With a passing thought that he hoped he would not plant his hands down on barbed wire, he followed round the edge of a large shell-hole. Warren knew the way fairly well and led on over comparatively easy going, but occasionally over a narrow, crumbling neck between two shell-pools. Twisting round one of these, Phizz lost sight of his guide. He stopped and looked round for him, but saw nothing on the broken outline of the hillside. The quiet crumbling of mud into still water caught his ear from behind him, and looking back he saw Warren sitting up and looking around for him. In some subtle way each realised that the other had seen him, and Phizz started to make his way round to Warren. He came up against a bunch of rusty wire, tried to work round it, and was faced by a long pool. He tried to get back again and found now that apparently the only passable path led further away from Warren. He stopped and considered the matter, vexed at being boxed up so quickly; then he marked his direction from the general outline of the ridge and worked towards where he knew the Pimple lay. After some time of devious crawling he came out in front of Warren, who quickly joined him. "Keep close," he whispered, then pushed on again. Now caked in soft mud, his legs soaked to the skin, Phizz began to feel chilly; but Warren was going slowly, moving quietly round one hole, then waiting in what cover he could get to listen carefully. A machinegun rattled out, and its note grew to a louder, sharper, higher crack-crack-crack as it swept over the two figures hugging the earth as low as instinctive self-preservation could force them. It receded and toned down as it swung away, then stopped abruptly. Away behind them a machine-gunner answered with a humorous attempt to tap out the time of a well known rag-time line in the ' Policeman's Holiday.' A dull red flash lit up the sky in front, then a long ten seconds afterwards a salvo of field-gun shell scurried over them to burst above the duckboards. A Boche sentry stirred up to his duty shot up a Very light - a stream of sparks and the swish of the cartridge made Phizz look up out of the hollow into which his body had sunk, but there was a disappointing nothingness: the light was a dud. Expectantly he listened for the next one, but the Boche was apparently not active-minded enough to go on, and none followed. Again they moved on, and saw a yard or two in front a low irregular bunch of wire, with thicker stuff standing up behind it. Warren looked round for his bearings, and edged up to the left. Suddenly there was a bang behind them and one of our 18-pounder shells swished down to burst over the Boche line just in front; then another, two more, another, another! Some battery was firing on the Pimple in retaliation for the rounds on the duck boards. Both officers were cowering down; high up behind a last bang lost itself in the spiteful ping of a short shrapnel burst: a series of soft splashes scattered round, and Phizz cursed bitterly his fellow gunners who had shot it. Then he noticed Warren turning back. "Is he funking it?" thought Phizz; when the other reached him and whispered, "They have got my leg. I can just get back all right, though." There was not a cry or a groan or anything; he just went back slowly dragging his leg. Phizz following saw him meet another shadow the sergeant, obviously - and stopped to think. Should he go on to the Pimple or go in? Warren could not want his help now that he had met the sergeant, and he decided to see the job through. He could easily recognise the rough outline of the Pimple, and reaching the belt of wire again, he lay flat and waited. After some time he recognised the sound of digging in soft earth; looking cautiously up, he saw vaguely against the sky a form working on top of the mound. He could hear frequent low whispers from behind it, and evidently a lot of quiet repair work was going on there. A louder voice spoke in a tone of authority; a determined tramp along wooden trench boards passed along, apparently in front of the mound, so the trench in front of it was probably still sound. The feet stopped, a pop, a trail of sparks from in front of the mound, and then a Very light sailed in the air above. Phizz was stretched flat, head on one side pressed on the ground. He waited quietly, but then his heart jumped. What were those two forms on his left, moving, was it towards or away from him? The light died out, and still he made out their outline as he lay rigid and tense, watching them with fascinated concentration. They moved, but which way? He clutched his truncheon. Had they seen him; would they see him if another light went up? If only he had a revolver, he would shoot and make it one for one anyhow! What an ass he had been! How long would they stay? - until day was nearly dawning and he was too late; or could they really see him now? Urgently he waited for the next light, so that fate might then decide; if they did nothing then, he would risk trying to get away. But which way was it that they were moving? Now - a light went up some hundreds of yards away. In that softer more distant light he recognised two old stumps; the apparent movement had been only the deception of his eyes in the fluctuating glare of the closer light.

Phizz decided this had been enough, and turned back. He was anxious now to get in as soon as possible and end his night's adventure. Almost carelessly he was splashing on as quickly as he could crawl, when he came to a sharp stop. A low cough had pulled him up fixedly. Where had it come from? Again a guttural cough, from the emptiness some yards to his right: in a flash Phizz knew that this was a German patrol; ignorant of his being alone, perhaps misled by his carelessness, they were anxious to avoid a clash out in No Man's Land which might easily mean death to both. Phizz very thankfully grunted his best approach to a low answering cough, and gingerly edged away. Safely he reached our wire at last, but here he had his final difficulty. How was he to cross it? - he knew of no practicable gap unless he could get along it to the place where he had started; crawling along the wire would be extremely difficult, for here was the most badly cut up ground of all; but his luck was in.

"Sir," an honest Cockney voice whispered from nowhere.

"Where are you?" Phizz whispered back. A hidden form rose slightly and beckoned Phizz; he followed and was soon led through a gap in the wire, and after a surprisingly short crawl they came in at the back of the picquet.

"Thank God you're in!" It was Williams' pleasant voice, in what sounded to Phizz like a cheerful bellow after the tenseness of the whispers in No Man's Land. "You're the last of the lot, and I was just hesitating about how much longer to wait before coming to search for you. Come along now at once to the dugout, both of you, and have something to warm you up." Phizz realised that his teeth were chattering and that he was intensely cold. "What time is it? Is Warren all right?" Phizz asked in one breath as they went down the trench.

"Oh, he's all right, the lucky devil! He has got the most priceless Blighty one. He is in the dugout now waiting to be carried out as soon as the relieving battalion have got in. They are relieving Centre and Left now, and should be here any minute. It is about half-past twelve, you know. Did you learn anything?"

"Yes, a little; and it was very interesting too. I am glad I went."

Near the dugout they met the head of the incoming relief. Slowly and tediously they made their way down, pressing into the wall and squeezing their way along. At last they reached the dugout, where Warren was lying white-faced, with a thick bandage round his thigh, but smoking.

"Good man!" he greeted Phizz, quite cheerily.

"I'm so sorry, old thing! How are you?"

"Oh, don't apologise I shall never have a bad word for our gunners again after their doing me so nicely for the England, Home and Beauty stunt. I only just got into the trench in time though, and I could not have done it if I hadn't left you at once. It is getting stiff now, but it doesn't hurt."

"Put this down you!" Williams gave Phizz and the man who had come in with him each a stiff tot of rum. "Here's luck to you and your damned guns!" He winked at Phizz as he took a drink himself. Then he added, "What about your clothes, Gunner? Have you any others here?"

"Oh, I have pyjamas here, and these things can be dried while I sleep, thanks."

"Pyjamas in the trenches ! Oh you - gunner!" he laughed. "Well, now I shall be busy handing over, so run down to battalion headquarters with your report. My signaller has already told them you are O.K. See you in Bruay on Sunday, then?

So long!"

"So long ! Good luck to you, Warren; and thanks awfully for the trip."

"Good luck, Gunner! Good-night." Warren's cheerfulness overcame the thinness of his voice.

Phizz went down to the battalion dugout. Crowded into the little room, on the bunk and the benches and the steps, were sitting the headquarter officers of both battalions, the incoming one including their doctor and assistant adjutant as well as the C.O., second-incommand and adjutant. They had already unearthed their supply of whisky, and the outgoing Colonel, with his mug filled and the prospect of rest from the trenches, had almost begun to feel pleased with life.

But he did his best to dispel the impression with his greeting to Phizz, when the latter's head appeared above the two officers who blocked the stairway.

"Here is our gunner, Dixon," he said to the relieving Colonel; "he has just wounded my best patrol officer with those infernal pip-squeaks of his. We are handing him over to you, as he only gets relieved to-morrow."

Phizz saluted and tried to explain that the guilty battery was not his, and that in any case such accidents were inevitable. But the Adjutant cut in, "That is the old story, Gunner; it always is some other battery. Well, what about the Pimple? Do you want to send a report through your own Brigade or through us?"

"Oh, it's your pigeon. You sent out the patrol; I will scribble a report such as it is, and you can do what you like with it."

"Right! Here is a message pad. Come inside!"

"Thanks very much," Phizz laughed sarcastically.

"Try our patent collapsible liaison officers: fold up into the smallest space: satisfaction guaranteed."

However, by a miracle of compression he was squeezed in between the two who already filled the stairway, and he gave his report of the condition of the Pimple. The Colonel took it and grunted.

"You gunners seem to have wasted your ammunition pretty thoroughly."

"Well, sir, at any rate it has not stirred up much retaliation on the duckboards. Did your battalion get through all right, sir?" he turned to Colonel Dixon. "Yes, thanks, so far as I know. There have been no reports of casualties as yet."

There followed a long and chilly time of waiting. The scattered odds and ends of papers and boxes of biscuits or cigarettes or notepaper, which had given the dugout its air of being comfortably inhabited, had all been cleared away. Only packed-up haversacks and equipment were left to emphasize the cold and bareness. At first the junior officers chatted with Phizz about his recent experience and the conditions of the trenches. Then there was nothing to do but wait for the company reports of completed relief. In long-protracted succession these came along. At last the final one was in; quickly the outgoing officers slung on their haversacks and with a few parting words of good wishes they climbed out, to go to meet their horses in Souchez.

Colonel Dixon pulled out from an attaché case a map of the trenches. Like almost every battalion commander who ever completed a relief, he grumbled about the amount of work on trench maintenance which the slackness of the other battalion had left for him to do. Then he called for his runner to go with him on a tour of the sector before the near approach of dawn should make it impossible.

"You have a runner who knows these trenches, sir?" Phizz asked.

"Oh yes, thanks. He came up last night."

"Then if there is nothing else you will want from me, I will turn in now, sir."

"All right! Only see that my adjutant knows where to find you. We shall have breakfast tomorrow about nine. Good night!"

"Good night, sir." Phizz went up into the trench. The chill of the hour before dawn, the darkness and silence unrelieved by any Very light or rifle report, brought home to him how cold and tired he was. Quickly he went into his dugout, and after a word with the telephonist sitting reading by candle-light, he slipped off his wet clothes and into dry pyjamas. He crawled into his sleeping bag on the upper bunk with as little creaking as was possible, so as not to waken the signaller snoring quietly underneath, pulled some of the clothes he had taken off over his feet for extra warmth, and dropped asleep.

CHAPTER V

A German attack.

A German attack is beaten off by artillery fire and by infantry defenders
-devastating effect of Minenwerfers -
many lives lost in the front line.

PROBABLY most readers have already a pretty true idea of "the Salient" as it was before the battle of Messines. Very roughly it was a half-saucer, with Ypres at the centre and the rim in Germany - three miles away. The central feature, though not by any means the highest point, was Hill 60. On the north the hill was isolated by a gap of nearly half a mile, which was so thoroughly dominated by the Hun sitting above it that we could not hold a line there at all, but defended it only from the flanks. Southwards the hill dropped away steadily for a thousand yards towards the canal, but its top was cut off from the rest by the deep cutting of the Menin railway. Some of the earth from the cutting was heaped up on the right hand side in two irregular heaps, of which, one was in our lines and the other "the Caterpillar," was Boche; but on the left had been heaped up a compact round which made the real Hill 60. Churned up by shell fire, torn by mine craters, it still dominated the southern half of the saucer; and more particularly, it looked down on the weedy 95 line of trenches sixty yards in front where the British were holding on by the skin of their teeth. But nothing could ever describe the eeriness, the menace of cruelty, which seemed to be embodied in that ghastly featureless heap. If you are squeamish about such things, do not try to picture it. But if you would know how terribly it could impress the imagination of those of us who had seen man after man heeled into that blood-soaked hill, think of the most ghastly scene you can conjure up; perhaps you have. seen the painting in one of the Bond Street galleries of the corpse of a ravaged Belgian girl, hacked into a red travesty of human shape, nailed to the door of a farm whose every window is spitting with a sniper's rifle; in front a few khaki figures are lying, helplessly squeezing down to cover from that stinging barrage of death. If you can clothe the grim picture of the hill with the horror of that scene, you may begin to know what it was like.

Phizz had seen it often, searching it through a periscope for any sign of life; but the best he ever saw was his own smashed periscope. He too had conceived a loathing for the sight of the hill, but partly it was dulled by concentrating on its details. However, now his duty was not here, but immediately south of the railway cutting, and he was no longer interested in the hill, except to keep out of sight of it. He was there as liaison officer to the centre battalion, commanded by Colonel Dixon.

"Good morning, sir. Am I late for breakfast?" he asked as he came into the mess dugout.

"Morning, Thurston. I thought you were rather early. Instead of being last as usual, you are only last but one."

Phizz laughed and sat down to the plate of porridge brought in to him. "That is the worst of going out to work before breakfast; you come in with those who never do any work at all," he added as the assistant adjutant came in.

"Swank!" the latter replied cheerily; "what work have you done? Have you killed any Fritzes? - no!"

"Well, like the man who didn't know if he could play the fiddle, I don't know that I haven't killed dozens. I had a shot at a Boche minenwerfer and burst one fairly close. But really, all our guns are so far back, and it is the very devil shooting at such long ranges. I wish they would let us have them further forward and risk it; the Hun couldn't give the battery a much worse time than he has given us already."

"The rashness of youth, my boy!" Colonel Dixon chipped in. "The Boche would simply blow you to hell if he had a stunt on, and then where would we infantry be?"

"Thank you, sir," Phizz made an elaborate salute. "Your good word for the poor old R.A. shall be written up over my bed in pink to match my pyjamas."

The Colonel laughed. "Compliments did not fly your way much a year ago, did they? I think it was that we never saw you getting shelled then, and we do see you getting it hot now: hotter sometimes than ourselves. It was 'the Somme' that made the difference."

"Yes, sir, that seemed to begin it, and it has been getting worse for us ever since. But I think you are going to get your share of it to-day."

The assistant adjutant, with a mouth half-full of bacon, contrived to whistle some bars of 'The Optimist and the Pessimist.'

"Kick him, Thurston, or sit on his head!"

The unappreciated humorist morosely finished his bacon.

"That reminds me, sir, did you hear about those Huns last night?" said Phizz. "No, what happened?"

"I was out about midnight on the bridge over the cutting, and from Hill 60 there was the most extraordinary chorus of Huns singing 'The Watch on the Rhine' and 'Vaterland' and so on, in jolly good tune too."

"In good tune! My voice reminded him!" interrupted the assistant adjutant.

Phizz went on: "They sounded very hearty about it, and I asked Brigade to strafe them; but they wouldn't on account of the relief of the Hill 60 battalion. They were afraid of retaliation."

"It would have been rather humorous if you had put a shell into the middle of the concert party. But just now you said you thought we should be strafed to-day. What makes you think so?"

"For one thing, that singing last night, sir. It isn't Christmas or the Kaiser's birthday or anything, so far as I know, and so at a guess I should think it must be the jolly old 'Storm-truppen' getting hearty. Then again, this minnying this morning."

"Yes, but your retaliation stopped that at once."

"I know, sir. But what struck me was the number of different ones firing, each of which sent only a couple of rounds; and as far as I could tell too, they were mostly new. It looks to me like registration for a strafe."

"Humm, I hope you are wrong, Thurston. This is no place to stand a bombardment. The trenches are nothing but tottering parapets, and there is only the one practicable communication trench. In any case we can't be allowed to clear the men out of the bombardment at all, for the front line is to be held as the main line of defence and hung on to at all costs."

"And what about us?" the assistant adjutant said, looking dubiously up at the roof. It was a lime-washed "cupola" dugout, of curved sheets of corrugated iron fitted together into a sort of section of the Underground Railway. They were on the same level as the trench, and above the roof was a bare two feet of earth and concrete blocks.

Phizz hummed the opening line of the 'Optimist and Pessimist.'

"That's all very well, Gunner," the other broke in, "but do you know what there is on this roof?"

"I saw three empty rum jars there yesterday," Phizz laughed; - "quite empty!"

"Well, you know too that there is no dugout yet finished which is any stronger?"

The Colonel interrupted. "It does show extraordinary lack of foresight that headquarters should be left here with so little work having been done on them. Yet I suppose the Boche knows what extensive mines we have under Hill 60, and if he wanted to go for anything would go for them, not us. But let me know if you see anything else, Thurston."

"Certainly, sir, I am going out again now, but I will be back for lunch." Phizz went out and along the front line, carrying out a close inspection of the Boche lines through his periscope without seeing anything new. There was practically nothing to be seen at all beyond their front line, which showed on the crest line some hundred and twenty yards away as a strong parapet of heaped bluish sandbags, pitched irregularly to help concealment of detail, such as loopholes. Our own front line was a more or less solid breastwork of bright sandbags, neatly and uniformly repaired in the many places where it had been knocked down. For the most part there was no protection behind at all, simply open ground. But there were occasional blocks of little cubby-holes, under low curved sheets of corrugated iron perhaps five feet across at the bottom and three feet high. These were blocked over with sandbagging, built up nearly to the height of the parapet. Inside these shelters a few men were curled sleeping or pencilling a mud-soiled letter home.

An irregular path of wooden trench boards, made as a sort of long wooden grating, led along the trench; but often a board would be so sunk in mud as almost to be lost. In some places another board had been laid on top of one so buried, and in walking along Phizz had to take care that the increased height did not bring his head above the parapet; at the same time the presence of short gaps and of loose boards which rocked up as one trod on them made it necessary to watch the floor just as closely. In each bay Phizz stopped to make his observation and to chat with the sentries about what the Hun had done in the night hours. All the men had somehow contrived to shave themselves; some were washing in old tins filled with water from one of the holes behind the trench. A young company officer came up and asked Phizz if he thought the Hun could see into the trench from anywhere, as at night they seemed to be machine-gunned almost from the rear. Cautiously Phizz drew back and showed the menacing mound of Hill 60 only just hidden by the winding of the parapet. The officer borrowed his prismatic periscope, and Phizz, leaning idly against the parapet meanwhile, noticed two men playing chess with a folding pocket board; both looked comparatively dirty and shiftless as against the noticeable cleanliness of most of the men, despite their mud-stained clothes. After a few minutes, Phizz and the other officer moved along to another bay.

"Do you keep chess champions in your battalion?" he asked.

"Rather!" the other answered. "Did you notice the one with glasses? He had his half-blue for chess. He came up with the last lot of conscripts we had. Poor devil, he is absolutely hopeless as a soldier, and will never get a stripe let alone a commission. There was another interesting fellow in the same section; I don't know whether you saw the man stitching a button on his trousers: he was the man charged in the Sixhills murder case, who just got off by the skin of his teeth. But he is no good either, for he hasn't a pal in the company."

"Have you many other 'celebrities,' or are those two the gems of your collection?"

"Oh, almost every man is interesting in some more or less striking way. I could go on talking to you for hours about them. One of our 'characters' is my batman, who is the Colonel's ground landlord at home. Our skipper's orderly is an ex-policeman; he was working a police trap that cost the skipper a fiver a few days before the war. Apparently they did some pretty hard swearing against each other then, but the two have been together through everything since February, '15."

"Gangway, please!" Two men with a glorified camp kettle between them interrupted them to pass by.

"Oh here is the men's dinner said the infantryman as they made way. "We have to give them three hot meals a day now, brought up in these new heat-retaining gadgets. I must go and give an eye to it, if you don't mind my leaving you."

Phizz asked if he might come along too. The sergeant had already begun distributing the hot and pleasantly smelling stew, ladling it out into the men's mess tins as they came along in turn. It was helped down in extraordinary ways according to individual taste. One man, for instance, took his mess tin lid full of pickles, and having gulped the stew, went on eating the pickles alone with great satisfaction. One mixed his ration of jam with it. In almost every case it was eaten quickly without any lingering over the meal as a relaxation; life for the men in a quiet trench is too entirely simple for that. With an edge on his appetite from the savoury smell of the stew, Phizz left the front line and walked back to headquarters for his own lunch.

"Enter Jeremiah the Second," the assistant adjutant called out; "do you still prophesy the fall of Jerusalem?"

"Sorry, old thing, my biblical knowledge isn't good enough to get the point."

"There is no point; but this morning you told us we were going to be blown into bits, and have we been? - no!"

"Well, touching wood and that sort of thing, I do seem to have been wrong," Phizz answered.

"Of course you are wrong. Thank the Lord you are a better shot than you are a prophet, Gunner ; Damn!" A hollow crash outside echoed in the ironarched dugout. Phizz went to the door to see where the shell had dropped.

"Pretty close to the reserve company dugouts, I think," he said, coming in again.

"Call for lunch, adj., and we'll get that inside us before anything nasty happens." Colonel Dixon drew his stool to the table.

Another crash outside: and a batman dived into the doorway with a rattle of crockery on the tray he was carrying. "Fritz is a-strafin', sir," he explained unnecessarily. The plates of cold beef were covered with fine black granules, and a smell of fusty matches hung about the room. Soon there was another burst, rather short this time.

"He is ranging, isn't he, Thurston?" asked the Colonel.

"It sounds rather like it, sir. Shall I ask for retaliation or would it be better to get counter-battery fire?"

"Counter-battery fire seems to be indicated, the sooner the better."

Phizz went out along the trench, ducking as he heard each round coming. Just outside his signallers' dugout he met one of them coming to tell him that the lines had been cut. He gave them some instructions and went to the infantry telephone dugout, where he got his message through over their line to the infantry Brigade. Coming back quickly to the mess dugout, he found the Colonel and Adjutant sitting silently in front of the untasted lunch.

"My lines have been cut near here, sir, and it does not look worth while to try to keep them through here; so I have sent the telephonists to tap into the line where it crosses the hedge, half-way down to the light railway. But I have asked for the counterbattery fire. Things look rather thick on the front, too, sir; and the whole Hill 60 sector is catching it."

"Yes, both my companies in the line are getting heavily minnied. Will you go and get retaliation on the Boche trench mortars. I have already sent to our T.M. man to retaliate on their lines."

Phizz took a biscuit with him. Outside he waited in the trench for a group of rounds to come over, then as soon as their splinters had whistled past he jumped out and ran over the open to the flank. Hearing another group coming, he dropped out of the way of their splinters and went on again to the place where he had sent his signallers. Clear of the line of shelling, with only occasional splinters sizzling past and burying in the soft earth with a 'phut,' the signallers were just connecting up. Phizz called up the Adjutant.

"Hallo! Thurston speaking, P.Y. 44. The Boche is strafing pretty heavily here with 'four-twos' and minnying the front line. I think he is knocking out the communication trench with 'five-nines' too. I'm sure all the Trench Mortar emplacements are new ones, as I told you this morning. Can you do anything?"

"Not much, Phizz," came the answer. "The left sector are getting it pretty badly too, and Divisional Artillery have asked the Corps Heavies to come in. They say they have an important scheme on this afternoon, and can only interrupt it if there is an S.O.S."

"What infernal stupidity, though! I'm quite certain the Boche is coming over as soon as he has flattened us out, and the time to stop him is now, not then. Can't the General do something?"

"He isn't in, Phizz, and the Brigade Major is helpless. We can put our own batteries on a slow rate of fire——"

"But you know how much use an 18-pounder is at five thousand yards, to smash up an attacking party in their trenches."

"Yes, Phizz, but I daresay it will be all right. These things always seem worse at the time you are getting strafed." The adjutant, who had been in a battery for one month in the days when the gunners' war was peace, was apt to take all reports for exaggeration. "But I say, Phizz, will you get on to our Trench Mortar battery; we can't raise them on the 'phone. See that they retaliate, and ask them this time to be more careful over their ammunition return afterwards. It makes an awful lot of trouble when the returns go wrong, as they always do on these occasions."

Phizz laughed sarcastically. "—And his casualty return: shall I check that for him, supposing that he can't? What is his full name, so that I can be certain of getting it right if he figures in it himself?"

"Thanks. I can correct details, if you will make sure it is complete." The answer came back in all seriousness.

"Well I'm ——" and he is not a bad fellow apart from business!" Phizz muttered to himself. Then speaking down the telephone again he went on: "Right-ho! and do get those heavies on if you possibly can."

"Yes, if I can. Let me know if anything more happens. So long!"

Phizz next rang up his battery and quickly explained the situation to Brown, who was on duty there. Then he pointed out to his signallers a little shelter which they could make use of a few yards further down, and walked back up the slope. In front of him, just over the breast of the hill, a steady succession of brown showers of earth were shooting up. On the left the communication trench running roughly parallel with the railway cutting was being traced with greasy black crumps which burst up with a shattering crash. Beyond was the Hill 60 sector, topped similarly with bursts, which in the comparative distance seemed remarkably fine and effective. Closer on his immediate left was the line of trees in the shadow of which lay battalion headquarters and the little shelters of the support company. The rest of the landscape was as clear and green as a shining spring afternoon could make it. A few khaki figures on the long stretch of light railway which led back towards Ypres were glancing up at the hill to watch the bursts of the bombardment, interested in the fine spectacle it made. One burst full on the trunk of one of the trees brought the top of it bodily down; Phizz saw two of these khaki-clad men pointing delightedly towards this very interesting sight, then hearing a swish in the air he ducked hard just in time to miss a great swinging branch which dashed down beside him. Looking back at the two figures, he realised that they were laughing at his hasty drop into the mud. Half-amused himself, half-depressed by the extraordinary isolation of it all, he went towards the headquarters. Choosing his moment he ran up to the trench and jumped in. Steadily the shells were dropping around in groups of four each minute, chopping up the earth into a patchwork of new brown holes; but extraordinarily little damage had been done to the trench, and none to the mess dugout, where the Colonel was still sitting by his wasted lunch. The peculiar rotten corpse-like smell of German high explosive hung strongly inside, and everything was powdered with those greasy granules of earth which are characteristic of fresh shelling.

"What luck, sir? You seemed to be having a pretty thin time these last few minutes."

"Pretty thin! But they seem to be concentrating on that line of shelters under the trees where I have my support company, rather than here. I am having them cleared out towards the railway."

"Well, sir, these shelters are in full view from near Hooge, up in the north of the Salient, and I should guess that this shoot is being observed from there. But all the ground down to the railway is equally exposed, so your men may not be much better off."

"Are you sure, Thurston? You suggested that once before, and I mentioned it to the G.O.C. and the 'G.S.O. one,' but they laughed at the idea."

"Well, sir, if it isn't lèse majesté to mention it," Phizz replied, "I don't think our staff are absolutely infallible about our own divisional front, let alone a neighbouring one. After Loos in 1915, one of them came up to our O.P. with the relieving general to show him the front. He pointed out Loos Towers all right, but mistook a slag heap in our line for the old Double Crassier, and after that bright effort just wound up, 'The rest of the front you will easily pick up for yourself.' As for this present position, only last week I went over to the Hooge front with a friend in a heavy battery, to watch him shoot at an enemy O.P. and from here you can recognise that O.P. quite distinctly."

Phizz paused for an instant, as a shell sounded as if it were coming on top of them but just swished over. "But the men would be out of sight in the hollow the other side of the hedge, and they would be out of the line of shelling too."

"Right, I will get out and have a look, but I shan't have to be long; for this is my fighting post, and I must stay here to keep in touch with Brigade. Did you get Heavies?"

"No, sir; they refuse to fire. Could your brigadier get the G.O.C. to ask for them?"

"I will try now." The Colonel buzzed on the 'phone beside him.

"I have to go and see our brigade trench mortar battery, the 60-pounders. I will get back as soon as I can." Phizz went out again. Quickly he got through the immediate danger zone, and taking advantage of the 'dead ground' to the right, he walked up to the breast of the rise to reconnoitre. A sunken road ran parallel with the line, and from here he had a fairly good view. A couple of machine-gunners were watching from the forward bank.

"Fritz is pretty lively to-day, sir," one of them said to Phizz.

"Yes, I'm afraid those minnies are giving our front line hell!"

"I've known Fritz knock 'em about worse than that, sir. Why, the night before last when the battalion on the right was raiding he went up and down this road with great big crumps, hitting it every time somethink terrible."

"Really? I once knew a man who had seen a worse strafe than any he had ever been in. He was in the A.S.C." But Phizz was too subtle for the machine-gunner, who with a polite "Yes, sir," went on with more details of the terrible night. Phizz was meanwhile watching the line with his field glasses. The communication trench on the left he soon realised was impracticable save as a last hundred-to-one chance. One man he saw try to jump over a block, and he dropped immediately to a sniper's rifle; while the whole of its length was being heavily basted by the Hun gunners. There was an old communication trench on the right, more or less derelict, and in a little off-shoot from this were the trench mortars he wished to reach. It was not being so systematically barraged, but sudden salvoes of 5.9 inch howitzers swept occasionally down on it as a series of heavy black crumps. The front line parapet was knocked away into a gaping hole about once in every thirty yards; there was no consistent barrage, but almost always in some part of the 500 yards of the battalion front an ugly black sausage-shaped can of explosive was being lobbed across, turning over and over till it fell; then an instantaneous pause, and a sheet of smoke would shoot out and curl in the wind with a shower of earth and debris raining down around it. Many dropped short of the trench and tossed long trailing bunches of wire entanglement into the air. Others fell on the blocks of cubby-holes and crashed them down into a crazily jagged cage of splintered iron. Others again burst behind and blasted every loose shred or trench board from the unprotected space behind the parapet. Of the garrison there was no sign save a few huddled figures of death. Back on the flank Phizz could make out groups of men of the right battalion watching this flattening out of their neighbour's trench - and of their neighbours. Their own battalion headquarters down in the woods on the flank were being heavily plastered too, but always there were the shining green fields behind emphasising the littleness, the isolation of those few acres of destruction.

Phizz made up his mind to a detour as far as the front line of the right battalion, and then to dodge the minnies if he could, along to the trench mortar dugout. He set off and quickly reached the nearest communication trench of the right sector, but along it his progress was very slow. Wounded being helped along by hand or carried on stretchers blocked the trench. It is no easy matter to carry the weight of a man prone on a stretcher along a narrow and winding trench; for those who try to get along in the opposite direction and yet avoid blocking the way down for the wounded, the going is slow and tedious. An occasional shower of shrapnel down the trench made it still worse. In one place two stretcher-bearers had put their burden down to rest themselves, and were now swearing at each other over the whitefaced, blood-splashed figure between them.

"I tell yer the —— is dead."

"An' I tell yer 'e was a groaning a minute ago and we've got 'im so far, we'll finish the job."

Phizz stopped their argument. He examined the torn body and said curtly, "He is dead now!"

"What did I tell yer! Now heave 'im up on top and clear the trench a bit. One, two, hup." Straining, they lifted the corpse over the trench and toppled it on to the ground out of the way. "Now we can go an' get someone as is alive." Phizz was going on again, but turned as he heard a shrapnel burst snarl close overhead. A dark trickle was spreading slowly over the sleeve of one of the bearers.

" 'Ere Joe, tie this up," he said, "and I'll be able to do one more journey afore it gets too stiff."

A few yards further up Phizz met the corporal of one of the trench mortar detachments who had originally been one of his own section in the battery; the man had been sent to trench mortars because of a general slovenly shiftlessness, but in the happy-go-lucky dirtiness of trench mortar work he had revelled and had made a little reputation for his fearlessness. He was now hopping gamely down on one leg, with the other foot hanging limply from the ankle.

"Hallo, Coggin, I'm sorry to see this," Phizz exclaimed.

"I'm not, sir. I'm *fini* with the war now, and it won't harm me in my civvy job at all"

"Good! But tell me what your guns are doing."

"Nothing sir; and won't do. Old Fritz he hit the bombs that we had fuzed, and the whole lot went into the biggest hole you ever did see, and only me hurt, sir, as we were all fetching more bombs from the little dump. Mr. Brooks was away with the Broken Tree guns at the time, and I sent the men there to help him and hopped down here myself. But it is a warm job; I never struck it so hot before. You want to be careful of the rninnies, sir; Fritz is doing fair hell with them."

"Gangway there!" A bearer was stooping under the weight of another man, whose legs were held up by a more lightly wounded man behind.

"Good-bye, Coggin. I hope you will get on well and save your foot."

"Good luck, sir!" The corporal began to hop on, but the pain of starting again after resting against the trench wall was too much for him.

"We'll see he's all right, sir. There's another man just behind me as can help 'im"; the sweating bearer stopped to ease himself, leaning against the side of the trench, and took in the situation at once. So Phizz went on once more and at last reached quicker going in the front line. At a corner he saw an infantry officer he knew, carrying a short stocky pistol such as a shot-gun cut off a few inches from the breech might make. A large red-capped cartridge was stuck in the end of it.

"Ready with the S.O.S.?"

"Rather, and I've got my Lewis gun in here to give the Boches a pill or two if they do try it"; he pointed to a little bay in which a detachment waited with their gun.

"Give 'em it strong, then," Phizz laughed, and crouching low, he dashed quickly along the battered line. Here and there was a body to be passed. One he thought he must have met before, and after some seconds recalled that it had been the chess player who was 'no use as a soldier and would never get a stripe.' In one or two bays where the parapet remained sound and the cubby-holes formed a parados, some tense-featured groups still hung on. A sergeant, recognising Phizz as he passed, called out, "What are our guns doing, sir?"

Phizz stopped and forced a cheery smile. "They are waiting to give Fritz an absolute burst of hell if he tries to show himself. They want to catch him absolutely on the raw, instead of just potting away at him while he is hiding in those dugouts and trenches"

"And what about us, sir?" One can pardon bitterness in a man who has been barely missed by the teeth of Death's horror and waits for it to drag over yet again and again.

"Well, you will give him hell too!" He looked the sergeant full in the eyes, and the man turned back to his bay, not with an answering smile but at least a better heart. Then, "Look out, sir!" he shouted.

Phizz watched the minnie roll over and over as it hung above them, then gathering speed lobbed wickedly down. He determined not to duck if he could possibly help it, and judging it closely, he edged a little further back in the angle of the traverse. For one breathless instant of suspended thought he felt he had misjudged it. Rigidly he held himself as he heard it bounce on the ground behind; then a deafening, head-splitting roar crashed through his ears and shook the earth he stood on. "You're not hurt, sir?" The sergeant still huddled in the trench carne towards him anxiously. The voice sounded faintly through the millions of cathedral bells rioting in Phizz's ears.

"No, rather not," he answered, spitting out the dust, "but I got a mouthful." He tried to force the blood back into his cheeks by will power, feeling that he was pale from the shock. His voice he felt too was very hollow, but he achieved a careless smile and strolled on with elaborate steadiness - and a very sharp eye open for another lobbing minnie.

He reached the old communication trench he wanted, and now went as quickly as he could; but that was a painfully slow scramble. The smashing of the sides had in many places jammed the revetment across the trench. In some places he could squeeze under, in others he could only crawl hurriedly over and drop hastily into the other side, hoping that he had not been marked down. Everywhere the blocking of drainage and the breaking of shell-hole reservoirs of pent-up water had flooded the trench nearly knee deep.

Some of the trench boards floated, others still stuck in the bottom. Every now and again a minnie would burst behind him; or with its Grroo-rroo-RROO-crash, clang, clang, a 5.9 would thunder its destruction in some part or other. At last he reached a sharp corner in the trench. Squatting in the water was a chirpy little Cockney corporal with about half a dozen men. "Here we are, sir," he called up. "Fritzy blew us out of the front line, so we are waiting for him here; and we'll catch him just as good, and safer."

"Oh, it is not you I am looking for; I am a gunner going to the trench mortars just further down. You do look comfortable!" Phizz grinned. "That's right, sir; it's ten to one against his hitting just this little corner, and if he does we won't know much about it. Is he coming over, sir?"

"Well, I don't know." Phizz looked doubtfully at the men trying to size them up. If you are looking forward to getting a shot at the Hun, I think you'll get it; but if he leaves the front line and tries to work up this trench, all I can say is he is a bit of a fool. Now can I get past you?" With much difficulty and a little good-humoured chaff, he splashed past or over them. In a few more minutes he reached the off-shoot which led to the first trench mortar emplacement. He called out "Toffee Apples!" the nickname of the 60-pounders. An answer came, but further down the trench itself. Phizz could see the splintered stump which gave this position its name of "Broken Tree." For the last few yards Phizz had to crawl over the top, but the ground was only exposed to Hill 60; itself wreathed in the smoke of the bombardment which was going on there. Crouched in the alley way leading to the second emplacement was a young bombardier with three men.

"Have you seen Mr. Brooks?" Phizz asked.

"No, sir, I want to see him. The last I heard of him, he went to see Corporal Coggin, and he hasn't got back. The Germans have buried the other gun and broken it up; and the water has come in here so that the bed has sunk and we daren't fire because it might go anywhere, in our trenches most likely; and I want to ask Mr. Brooks what we can do. I daren't go back without him telling me, and we are doing no good here."

"Will your gun fire at all, if you get set on the right line again?"

"Oh, yes, sir; she's the best gun we have, and a beautiful bed she had, sir, if it hadn't been for this water all draining in."

"You are quite sure the water won't stop you firing?"

"No, it's not high enough for that. But it's no use, sir, we might just as likely kill our own men as the Fritzes."

"Quite - what few are left to kill," Phizz muttered; then continued, "Now I think I can register for you on the Boche front line. If I do that, will you carry on as long as you can, sweeping about a bit. I will choose a place so that it will be safe to do so. You haven't been shot at so badly recently, have you?"

"Not this last half-hour."

"Then do that, and I'll bet you a fiver to an old tin hat that you have a Military Medal at least stuck on you when next you take your girl to the pictures. You have a rifle and some ammunition?"

"Here, sir."

"Right! Now I am going to crawl along that hedge at the back to a place where I can see the Boche line. You send off a bomb, and if I fire low over you it means drop a bit, if I fire high add a bit, if to your right go a bit to the right, and similarly left. Three rounds rapid will mean O.K., carry on. You won't be likely to mistake it in spite of the racket, for a bullet fired close past you doesn't leave you much room for doubt. I shan't be able to come back, as I have been away too long already. If the Boche should attack, you can drop comfortably a hundred yards and blow him up in No Man's Land without touching our own trenches."

"Yes, sir. We'll be all right, and ready by the time you are."

"Good man!" Phizz took the rifle and crawled away along a thin hedge, trusting to the smoke and the lowering afternoon sun to conceal him. Very soon he had reached a point where just over our own broken parapet he could see the low line of the German wire. At the same time he heard the "pop" of the mortar, and a great round ball with a long steel tail dangling from it, shot up into the air, poised at the top of its flight and curved gracefully down to pitch badly short and burst in our own wire. Phizz fired up in the air above the emplacement. After some delay an answering bomb soared up and burst just in front of the German parapet. That was good enough, and he let off three rounds quickly into the blue. Another bomb followed almost immediately, and he watched interestedly to see if it would burst near the same place.It dropped out of sight, and for an instant he thought it was a dud. Then a beautiful burst shot up out of the trench, hurling a bit of scaling ladder high into the sky. Phizz fired three more rounds, and calling out a vain message of farewell which was lost in the steadily increasing noise, he crawled through the hedge and bolted over the open for the hollow below in which he would be out of sight. He reached that security and walked as quickly as he could over the open fields to get to battalion headquarters.

Within sight of it he stopped for a moment. He knew he had not lost his way, but what he was making for was almost unrecognisable. The trees were now a row of gaunt white trunks, stripped of all branches, and splintered so that hardly any bark was left. The ground, which that morning had been green field, showed now no standing blade of grass, no relief at all from its monotonous brown of newly-turned earth drying in the sun. Without any expectation of finding a standing dugout, he hurried along towards where the headquarter mess should have been. The trench near it was still intact, though full of loose earth above the trench boards. The top of the dugout showed no hole, only an added covering of this finely-broken earth. An arriving shell made Phizz jump for the door. Inside sat the Colonel, still beside his untouched plate of spoiled beef, almost as though in the dugout time had stood still in the crowded hours which had passed for Phizz since he left it.

"I have just been speaking to your C.O., Thurston," he said in a matter of fact way. "He seems to have done what he could, but if I had that Heavy Artillery commander here, I should stick him up for my own men to shoot at!"

"There is no doubt at all that the Boche is coming over, sir." Phizz began to tell of the scaling ladder episode, but Colonel Dixon cut him short.

"Any idiot can see that! Such an afternoon as this had been does not lead to placid conversation. "Your C.O. says all his batteries are getting drenched with gas, but they will be able to support us all right."

"Yes, sir, I could hear the shells going over towards our batteries. I think the shelling is thickening too, over the front. I will watch outside for an offensive barrage opening up, and the instant it does I will ask you if I shall send the S.O.S. Will that do sir?"

"No, don't wait to ask me. I know you are one of our old hands, and I'll be responsible for your sending it as soon as you think the thing is beginning. All my lines to the companies have gone, but I must remain here. The second-in-command tried to get through to the front line, but the trench is absolutely impossible. He is with the support company just at the back. The reserve company is coming up. Get out now."

"Right, sir." A quickening of the rate of fire of the battery which was plastering the area of battalion headquarters hurried his steps. Near where he had posted his signallers he paused to look round. Still there was the same smiling afternoon sun shining over the greater part of the landscape, but the successive crumps and explosions on the front continued unabated. Turning back he saw the support company deployed in the hollow, lying down beside their arms. Suddenly the quick bark of field guns rattling out a barrage broke into the intermittence of the deliberate destructive fire. All along the front a hail of shrapnel and the heavy pounding of a hurricane bombardment with trench mortars told of the barrage which was to roll the way clear for the assault. Phizz had the momentary satisfaction of seeing the "Toffee Apple" shoot up once more out of the smoke; then he hurried down to the signallers.

"S.O.S." he shouted out. But already there were two or three floating red lights over the smoke on the front, and the waiting artillery barked into its answering barrage; its effect, however, was hidden behind the dense rolling barrage of the enemy. A line of black crumps leaping up on the breast of the ridge and stretching down the communication trench, came slowly on towards the hollow. Hill 60 was completely hidden in smoke. The battalion on the right was cut off by an intense barrage of high explosive, and blinded by a wall of artificial smoke. Machine-guns everywhere were cracking continuously. The waiting figures in the hollow watched the line of shells creeping down to them, watched for a line of grey-clad Huns to appear on the skyline. Now a battery began to crump the light railway behind them, and they lay there in between two fires. Most of the men were quipping each other as they waited, safe so far and rather fed up with lying about.

"Give me an attack any day, you do get your rum ration," Phizz heard one say; "but bein' attacked is no bon!"

"You wait a bit, my lad, and we'll go in for some of Fritz's ration if he's brought any across with him," his sergeant called out.

"Fritz don't have no rum."

"Well he has brandy."

"He don't. He has meffylated spirits." The argument went on light-heartedly. Still the field-grey uniform did not show itself, and the barrage no longer drew nearer but was getting ragged.

Phizz rang up brigade to tell them what little he knew of the situation as yet, before leaving to do some reconnoitring. As he was speaking he saw some of the infantry below being led leisurely up the hillside in little scattered groups. They got through the barrage with only a few falling, and had disappeared. Phizz went back to see the Colonel.

"You are counter-attacking, sir?"

"Yes, Brigade have ordered it on both battalion fronts at the same time. I can't make out any rifle fire, so I think the Boche must have cleared."

"I will just warn the batteries not to shoot too fine with their S.O.S. now, sir." Phizz hurried off with his message that the Boche was probably back in his own line now; and then returned to Colonel Dixon again.

"Any news, sir?"

"No!"

"May I go and see what has happened?"

"No, wait until things are more settled."

So Phizz waited until it was almost dark, when only a very thin remnant of the barrage was still pounding in occasional scattered rounds over the whole front. Sudden salvoes dropped irregularly round the headquarters, but the shooting was now erratic, and the dugout having come miraculously through so much without being hit, seemed almost comfortably safe. The railway was catching most of the shelling now. A runner came in with a message that we were back in the front line, having only just seen the tail end of the Boche raiding party as they withdrew. Phizz got permission now to go up, and went at once over the open towards the "Toffee Apple" emplacement.

It was dark enough now to be safe, and the area so recently torn by the barrage had become as quiet as any part of the front. Heavy shelling rumbled past overhead, but this part of the scene of the raid was left alone. The stench of smoke and H.E. was powerful, but it was clearing. Phizz stumbled his way along the top of the trench towards the emplacement and missed it. Going back he found the broken tree, but the emplacement had disappeared; so he went on towards the front line. He recognised the corner where he had passed the cockney corporal and his men, but no one was there; some yards further down he fell over a heap of

German 'potato-masher' bombs on to the body of a dead Hun, so the enemy had at least reached so far. In the front line he found an officer looking after his platoon as they cleared the trench and were building up the parapet.

"How did it go?" Phizz asked.

"Oh, pretty dull; no fight you know!"

"Any of our fellows left in the front line?"

"No, only these deaders, and most of them done in by the bombardment, not by the attack. The Hun tried to work down the trench there, but a corporal and a few men held him up. They say the Boche collared a few prisoners out of the front line, mostly wounded; but they certainly shot a good many of the Huns; so that even if we have lost the best part of two companies in casualties, he may not have scored so much on the deal."

"Is the corporal you spoke of still all right?" Phizz asked.

"Oh, yes; he is in charge of the next bay there."

Phizz found the little Cockney; "I'm glad to hear you did so finely, and held the Boche up," he said.

"Thank you, sir. I felt we was all right in that corner, somehow. He tried all he knew, too, to get us and that Toffee Apple, but when his barridge went back we just sat up and picked 'em off like sparrers. They took some of the men as were left in the line withaht a fight, for they hadn't a charnst, sir; they was too many. Then Fritz tried to come and bomb us and we just copped 'em nicely; so they stopped and tried to shoot us, showing more sense, but just afore he had any luck the whistle blew full time and his barridge came back, so he had to hop it. And we are still all right, sir, none of us hurt."

"Good man! and what about the Toffee Apple?" "Ah, sir, he was wonderful, he was; fair spifflicated 'em, he did; just knocked 'em down like skittles every time. But something must have happened, for after the barridge had gorn away he just blew himself up, like. Poor feller, after all them shells the Germans missed him with, and him stickin' it brave as can be !"

"Well, you both deserve a V.C., and I would be glad to see you get it."

"Thank you, sir. Same to you, and many of 'em!"

Phizz was not quite sure whether this was serious politeness or native humour. He shifted to surer ground by wishing the corporal a quiet night for his digging.

Once again Phizz strolled down the trench as he had done eight hours before; almost it seemed that an unreal nightmare had been seething in his brain, and he had just waked up again; but the few still forms not yet cleared away had had the nightmare and would not wake up. He reached the edge of the right battalion and learned how the dense barrage over the dividing line had stopped all the help they had hoped to be able to give to the other battalion. They asked how many casualties there had been, and offered some wild guesses. Phizz went on, and half-way down the trench stopped to let two men carrying cookers go by. Another hot meal was going up now, by a different route, and to different men, but that was all. The General ordered three hot meals a day. The General ordered the line to be held at all costs; and to-day the General's orders were not doomed to be thwarted.

So Phizz got back to the headquarters. His own little dugout had gone west, but all the officers would be able to sleep in the Mess, and his blankets had been retrieved from the debris. Supper had already been served, and the batman brought in for Phizz a plate of cold beef! Phizz had last seen him when he came hurriedly into the dugout shaken and white. Now he was quietly waiting on him as he might have done at Simpson's, or perhaps rather in Wardour Street.

The next morning Phizz received orders to carry out a shoot which could only be satisfactorily observed from a point on Hill 60, near the front line. At breakfast he spoke of this.

"You won't have much luck, I'm afraid," the adjutant remarked; "They have only two posts in the front line there now, according to what I heard this morning; and all their trenches are blocked, so all your wires will certainly have been cut."

"I expect so, but I am going to run a new line temporarily from the buried cable at the headquarters, along Marshall Walk - the trench running up the side of the Cutting, you know."

"Do I not know; - the filthy stinking death-trap!"

"Yes, it always was unhealthy, with the Boche fizz-banging right down it, and minnying it, and then crumping the back end of it for a change; but it seems quiet enough this morning."

"I wish you joy of it. But if you want to go and get killed, why not do it comfortably in our own sector here? Our padre gives you a top-hole funeral, and I'm sure he would spread himself on you."

"Thanks awfully! The ceremony will take place quietly owing to the war. No cards will be sent, but all friends are invited. Tear gas will be provided free of charge. Aren't we cheerful this morning? I'll see you again at lunch." Phizz went out to get a telephonist and what equipment he needed.

After crossing the railway cutting at a point further back under the breast of the hill, Phizz and the signaller walked up it as far as the mound known as Larch Wood, inside which the left battalion headquarters were safely tunnelled. There 'Marshall Walk' began, and they went along the trench. It was nowhere completely blocked, but everywhere pretty thoroughly battered, stinking of rotten sandbags and death, and the foulness of the water-logged cutting below; further up it was still worse, where the retiring Boche had left little gas bombs behind him. There was not a man to be seen, alive or dead, until nearing the end Phizz looked down one of the shafts of the mine system which we had cut into the hill. A few men were sitting on the gallery steps.

"Is there an officer down there?" Phizz called.

There was not, so he asked what they were doing. "Waiting to help clear out the mines," they answered.

"The Hun got down here, then?"

"Aye, sir, but the tunnellers soon kicked him out, and they're starting work again now. There wasn't much damage done."

Phizz went on to the head of the trench. There he found a group of bombers posted; they were talking, it seemed, of the Divisional Concert Party. He passed them, and after a few yards in which the trench was curiously intact, he came to a dead block where a huge minnie had thrown a wall completely across it. But the point he wanted to reach was several yards further along; and seeing a thin curl of smoke rising, he guessed that there must be someone there. Pulling his tin hat well down over his eyes, he raised himself with cautious slowness until he could just see over the trench. An accident of conformation made it just possible to get across without being exposed except to the very top of 'the Caterpillar'; worth risking if done once only, and done quickly. Telling his signaller to wait for him, Phizz wormed his way over, flattening himself down as low as he could. Slipping head foremost down the other side, he found the smoke rising from the timbers of a wrecked dugout! Slightly annoyed at having been so badly had, Phizz went on a couple of yards to an angle in the trench, but with a jerk he stopped. A German lolling drunkenly against the traverse was winking at him with his tongue stuck out. In an instantaneous flash he realised that he himself was unarmed, and on the top of it that the figure was dead. Shocked in spite of himself, he stood as far from the dead Hun as he could, and putting his periscope up under cover of a coil of wire, he looked beyond the traverse towards the point he wished to reach; he realised almost gratefully that it was absolutely impassably blocked. He would go back and try the only other part of the hill with the necessary view, a rather exposed position on the hog's back which ran away from the top to drop down to Zillebeke village. Looking cautiously back across the block he had crossed, he caught four pairs of eyes glued on his head with the sparkle of very close interest. They were the bombers who, some fifteen yards away round the bend of the trench, looked across at him from behind the rough heap of sandbags which hid them from the enemy.

"There is no other way to get out of here, is there?" Phizz asked.

"No, sir," one of them answered decidedly. Then after a pause, while Phizz was marking down the last inch of concealment he could get, the bomber went on: "Fritz killed our officer there an hour ago, sir; through the head."

"Good Lord!" Phizz ejaculated. He knew he ran more risk the second time than the first, but he had at least been certain that he would be only half exposed, and that only to the point high on the Caterpillar which he hoped no one would venture to use except for a target thoroughly worth while.

"Yes, sir," continued the bomber, "we was watching you go over, never expecting to see you get to the other side."

Perhaps they only guessed that Phizz was going over when they saw him begin, and it was too late to warn him. At any rate the thing was done, and no good was to be gained by cursing them.

"You know the Germans is only eighty yards away, sir?" one of them continued.

"Sixty, to be exact; it is not those just over the way I'm worrying about, though, but the perfect little gentleman across the other side of the railway.

However, I can't stay here all day; here goes!" With a little more haste and less cautiousness he flopped over, keeping his head well down, but less successful with a perhaps more conspicuous part of his anatomy. With a relieved sigh he picked himself up safe and sound from the floor on the right side of the block, to meet the four bombers laughing quietly at the ungainly figure he had cut.

"I'm going now," he said to them, "and I hope I shan't have drawn any rifle grenades down this way. Good-bye!" With a glint of amusement at the shadowed faces of the bombers, as only half-seriously he had mentioned rifle grenades, he strode down the trench followed by the telephonist. Reaching Larch Wood they went through the headquarter tunnels and came out on the far side of the mound. "You stay here, fix up a line to this side, and I shall be able to signal down to you for the shoot; for I can drop under cover of the hill," Phizz instructed his man, and then picked his way over the hillside.

If you know what it is like to drag through thick blue clay, soaked to the consistency of fresh putty, churned up by shells and cut into deep holes by trench mortars, then you will understand why it took Phizz a long five minutes to move a hundred yards over the desolate hillside. At last he reached the old support line, and stopped in absolute amazement. Not a hollow, not a sandbag, not a trenchboard remained to show that there had once been a line there at all. In one place only was a dilapidated relic of the revetment, and that was all: elsewhere, the same churned-up, glutinous mud as the stretch he had crossed. Away on the right a dejected tunneller was hauling up greasy sandbags from an invisible shaft and running them along a little wooden railway which had been set working again. On the left the line of the trench became again recognisable, and in places was quite clear. But here for two hundred yards it had disappeared in the most complete and effective obliteration Phizz had ever had the surprise of meeting.

He struck out for the hog's back further along.

The trench on which he had relied for concealment having vanished, he cut round by ground which brought him only into view from too great a range for rifle-sniping. Some angry fizz-banging searched for him, but too late, as he had doubled round again under the slight ridge he wanted to reach. Some broken mounds remaining from the parapet of an old communication trench offered the point of vantage he needed, and crouching he approached these.

"You want to keep low there, sir," a man leaning back against one of the mounds called out. Phizz had not noticed him, with hands and face and clothing stained with the same mud as his background.

"Why, where do you think the Germans are?" Phizz asked.

"Somewhere round here," he waved a comprehensive sweep around the sky-line over the hill.

"Do you know you are in view where you are, and I am not?"

"No, sir." He slipped lower down the mound with the air of one just changing his position for greater ease. "But I know Fritzy is just back here," he went on jerking his thumb back towards the top of Hill 60.

"Yes, you need to be careful about showing yourself there."

"You do that, sir; and that's what I told this silly bahstard here, but he must go and see for 'isself." As Phizz reached him the man pointed down to a body at his feet with a neat little hole in his forehead, and a horribly shattered head behind. "Aye, he caught it proper, he did," the man went on, "and serves 'im right for not takin' notice of what's told him."

Phizz had that reserve of mental resilience which the previous years had forced on him, but the ghastly callousness of the living man and the gaping head of the dead almost sickened him. Calling up his chilliest detachment of mind, he looked rigidly away and chose a suitable mound for his observation. Dropping down behind it, he signalled down to his telephonist at Larch Wood; and forgetting the infantryman, he carried on with the shoot. It was not a long business, but enough to give him back his natural cheeriness in the success of the shooting. When he finished, the infantryman, who had looked on at his antics in signalling without much interest, was cutting out chunks of bully from a tin with his jack knife, and helping it down with rather dirty biscuit. Seeing Phizz packing up his gear, he asked, "Sir, have you got any dinner with you?"

"No, I'm afraid not, or I would be glad to give you something to help your bully down."

"I don't want nuthink, sir; I thought you would like some. You can have his share." He pointed his knife at his dead comrade.

"Thanks, I shall have plenty when I get back. Haven't you some others here with you?"

"Yes, sir, just up there a bit there's some more, but I think I can manage it, if you don't want a bit."

Phizz left him emptying the tin. An hour later he was back at lunch. "Have a good time, Gunner?" the Adjutant asked him as he came in.

Phizz took a long strong whisky. "Yes, rather!" he answered; "it was one of the luckiest shoots we have had up here; I'm very glad I saw it through. But," he added, "if I ever have a nightmare, Hill 60 will be in it."

CHAPTER VI
The Somme.

Moving off from a French village -
brigade takes part in an early attack before the main Somme offensive -
tension before going over the top.

On a fine summer morning of 1916, a score of motor 'buses lined up in the streets of a French village. Two years before, any one of them might have been seen trundling down Piccadilly or disappearing towards Chalk Farm, flaunting the advertisements of Absolutely Pure Cocoa, or 'A Little Bit of Fluff.' Now their broken windows were boarded up with old box lids, the bright red of the 'General' was hidden under a heavy coat of W.D. green, and altogether they had sobered down and aged under the strain of war and French pavé. But the jolly crowd of Cockneys who filled them, instead of being sobered, were like a rollicking red-faced party of schoolboys out for an annual treat. They swarmed upstairs and down again; re-arranged their kit-bags inside the 'bus; ran from one to their friends in another; or stood on the steps outside to impersonate the conductor.

"Shepherd's Bush, lady? Change at Tipperary for Leicester Square, twopence all the way. Fares, please!" and the conductor's bell clanged into the chorus.

"No good, Leicester Shquare! You want chocolat, des oranges, d'p'tits gateaux, monsieur?" Mademoiselle was holding up in her sturdy arms a market basket filled with the curious assortment of sweetmeats which Tommy loves.

"You come with us, Mamselle. You come inside, chèrie."

"You no good! plenty piccaninny, you!"

"You fiancee, Mamselle? Et combiang les pommes?"

"Deux sous, monsieur, de belles pommes! C'est pour combien? Trois? Merci bien, monsieur. Et du chocolat?"

The same light-hearted banter, the free spending out of quickly emptied pockets, the same hard-headed business instinct mixed up with it by the French villagers, was being enacted round each of the old 'buses. Officers were strolling up and down chatting to each other or wandering off to the fruiterers round the corner for their own light lunch: or suddenly remembering some omission and hurrying along with a great air of important business on hand as they made through a crowd of Tommies to find one of their sergeants to set it right. Then a murmur slipped down the column, there was a rush for seats upstairs, a great winding of starting handles; the leading 'bus grated into gear. A confused cheer filled the streets, and each 'bus in turn jerked forward.

"Bonne chance, messieurs! A bas les Boches! You come back soon." The ladies picked up their lightened baskets.

"Apray la guerre, Lizzie!" and a rafale of popping kisses blew down from the side of the 'bus. Heartily the ladies waved them back, then jumped out of the way of a puffing figure who dashed after the 'bus which was leaving him behind. From a juicy paper-bag in each hand he was dropping squashed plums as he ran, to a chorus of cat-calls from his friends in the 'buses. Then with a heavy scraping of brakes the convoy pulled up a couple of hundred yards ahead, to stand there for another half-hour and the whole act began again.

At last the Adjutant and the Brigade SergeantMajor came down the column; they collected reports from each battery commander, and the SergeantMajor gathered in the stragglers with a few well-chosen words in the style of Pygmalion and the voice of a bull. There was a last chorus of banter and whistling and cheering, and the 'buses were really off. A crowd of little children just out from school ran alongside and fought for the pence and the oranges tossed down to them, or dashed off on a false scent after a fallen plum-stone. The air of 'I want to go home' rose out of the medley of noise, and finally drowned it.

XYZ Brigade were setting out to battle.

The officers of C Battery sat on the front seats of one of these old 'buses, with the exception of Brown, who was ahead with the transport at the village where it was now to be caught up by the gunners. They were speculating as to their eventual destination. There was of course no doubt they were to be thrown into the battle of the Somme, but into what part of it? Gurney was examining a map in the 'Times' as well as the lurching 'bus would allow him, and trying to make out which was the most crucial part of the new salient. Of course that was where the division would go, for such a first-class fighting unit must needs be given the hardest task. Phizz agreed with the thesis, but refused to follow it further, for sufficient unto the day was not his particular evil.

"What do you think of it, Major?" pursued Gurney.

"What? Oh, the war, you mean. I was thinking of the dust these 'buses kick up and wondering if the men in the back 'bus were enjoying themselves. You are both grey in the face already, and I expect I am too."

They laughed at each other under the film of dust, and then the Major reached across for the map.

"This sort of thing is dashed little use," he went on. "I have been trying to get to the bottom of that last battle, and I can't make head or tail out of it. All the papers make out that we won a magnificent victory and that sort of thing. None of us knows a word more than was in them, and personally I don't believe any of it."

"But surely, Major," Gurney continued, "our people are never allowed to put in these official accounts stuff that is literally not true?"

"Perhaps not," Major Osborne answered reflectively. "But it will take a great deal to take out of my mind what happened at Loos. You had not joined us then, Gurney, but you were in the 'Ammunition Column,' and you can remember how for three days you were kept standing under harness ready for the dash forward, with your map marked with watering places for the horses, nine miles deep into the German line. You saw the pitiful weariness and rawness of the reserve divisions that came up past your horse lines, the confusion and congestion that filled miles and miles of the roads to Noeux-les-Mines with a dead block of men and transport hopelessly and inextricably wedged. That was one side of it. I saw myself that forlorn and gallant struggle over Hill 70. I saw the remnants of a company surrender on the crest, after being shelled throughout the day by both sides. I saw our own Infantry Brigadier lunching under Lone Tree with a table and a white table-cloth, to try and put heart into the reserves on our flank, who were broken almost before they reached the line. And I came back over bridged trenches marked with sign-boards 'Cavalry track A' and 'B' and 'C,' and so on; past the bleached grass where our own gas had drifted over our own lines when we started off in the morning. Then Brown met me, and told me he could not replenish our ammunition, and you in the Ammunition Column had none you could supply. And so it went on till three days later we were relieved at the cross-roads near Noeux-les-Mines I bought the 'Daily Mail,' and opened it there. In great block letters across the whole centre page was this one headline, 'VICTORY.' Just then I heard the pipes, and the poor old Fifteenth Division came swinging by, relieved like us; marching, as fine a set of men as ever swung a kilt behind a pipe band. I thought it was a company, but it was a battalion, followed by another band and another tartan with barely a hundred yards from pipe-major to pipemajor. And I stood with that paper in my hand and watched them wind up the hill, battalion after battalion, slowly and grimly trudging by to the eerie skirl of mingling pipes that still drifted on the wind as they disappeared in succession over the crest. That picture has made the deepest impression on me that any in the War is likely to do. A few months later, you remember, Sir John French's dispatch was published. It almost convinced me that I was mistaken, and it really had been a success after all. Perhaps it was. I only know what I saw. Since then I no longer try to find out what has happened. The war correspondent's blarney is about as useful as Aunt Thingummy's corner in the Nursemaid's Own Journal. The communiqués are as likely to tell you what we were really trying for and what it cost us, as they are to tell the Hun just where our battery position is. Just now, I'm much more interested in the billets waiting for us to-night."

"You know, Major, I believe you think we are losing this jolly old war instead of winning more miles now from the Boche than we ever have done before," Thurston chipped in.

"That's rot, Phizz. Of course we shall win: because we have damn well got to go on till we do; and if I did think we were taking a knock I wouldn't dream of letting you fellows think the same. But we shall have to fight it out, not do any wonderful stunts to finish the war in a day. That is what you must be prepared for; but so long as you kill a Boche when you have the chance and don't let him get you first, that is all that matters to you. We don't know when a 'victory' is really a victory and when it isn't. I'm not trying to make out that every victory is really a defeat. Only it is beyond us, and it is no use our worrying about it anyhow. Now shut up about the blessed thing and look at the scenery, or have a banana or go to sleep."

"——This is topping country we are getting into, isn't it? These green hills and valleys are a bit of a change from the old slag-heaps." The irrepressible Phizz had caught the Major's mood at last.

The rolling hills crowned with green woods, and crossed by fine avenued roads, were full of that rural beauty which none can ever hope to drink in as can the man whose trade is destruction, leaving behind him the desolation he has helped to make. One can feel the refreshment, the comfort of it all, with a satisfaction one had never dreamt of before. For the moment the convoy was running along a terraced road below which a delightful little brook wound through the valley and lost itself beneath the trees and roofs of a prosperous village. There is no more placidly delightful picture on which to rest the eyes and mind than such a French village. One need not be temperamental to feel a new life springing up, new strength. When divisions are being "fattened" for a battle the Army spends much valuable transport in getting them to scenes such as this, for the spirit and zest which they gain there is real and of untold value. For XYZ the "fattening" was beginning. The whole afternoon they were being carried back through such country, through villages where church bells rang, past fields where the women looked up from their labour to smile at the unwonted sight of khaki. Soon every man in the convoy had cast out of his mind the war they had left behind. They were back into peace.

Now a word-painter like Hugo could spend hours in writing of the beauties of rural France and come no nearer to the spirit of them all than that single word, Peace. We shall not pretend to describe the placid variety and charm of the scenes through which men passed to the country of the Somme, but leave the reader to assume them as part of the atmosphere in which these Cockneys were to live and march until once more they turned their heads east to the battlefield. On this first day they travelled at the slow pace of a motor convoy until just as everyone began to wonder hopefully if tea would be ready for them when they arrived, the 'buses all pulled up on the roadside.

"Dismount! kits out !" the order passed back from 'bus to 'bus.

"What's the joke?" grumbled a man on a back seat as the leading 'buses emptied and it was clear that they really had to get out and unload on the side of this country road apparently miles from any shelter. As soon as all were clear the old 'buses rattled on and disappeared. The officers shared in the general amazement at this extraordinary treatment.

"Another mistake by the Staff Captain, I expect!"

The Major stretched himself after the ride and walked away to find the Adjutant. Meanwhile on the bank beside the road appeared the long, lean form of Brown

"Hallo, Brownie, old thing! I've never been so glad to see you for years and years," called Phizz. "I thought we had been dumped here in the middle of nowhere, to sleep in the ditch and eat raw turnips."

"And you thought your beloved Capting would desert you? Never!"

"Well, hardly ever, so far. But what about it now?"

"Oh, 'buses can't get into the village without going some miles round to the main road. We shall go down that side lane ahead, and get there in a quarter of a mile. And I say, old bird, such billets! and such a Mess! —eggs and milk and Madame's coffee, and her own wine, and fresh vegetables and fruit off the trees, and any other blessed thing you'd get in Arcady."

"Don't, Brownie ! You can't think how hungry we are."

"Then there's fresh trout for dinner, and apple meringues, and salad and anything else you can think of and ask Madame to make." Brown grinned and ducked as Phizz threw a clod of earth at him. Just then, however, the Major returned, and Brown, saluting, reported that a wagon was coming along for the baggage, and that he was ready to guide the whole party of the battery to their billets in the nearest farm of the village. Quickly the men were formed up and marched in, where not only was tea waiting for them, but also the mail from home, delivered there by some mystery of organization to give the last touch of pleasure to a perfect situation.

After tea all the officers strolled down to the horse lines, which were in a paddock alongside a broad stream. The men were already bathing in the clear water below, and Brown said he knew of a pool just further along where one could swim in comfort. Towels were sent for and the four of them were soon revelling in their first real bath for months. A wonderful Frenchman whose fishing they had spoiled for the evening came and clapped his hands in admiration - luckily they knew enough French to recognize his excited volubility for what it was, without mistaking it for abuse at the loss of his evening's sport. He begged them to remain while he fetched his daughter to see this extraordinary game of the brave English sporting themselves in the cold fresh water, really on purpose and not through the accident of having fallen in. The embarrassing prospect promptly finished their swim, and they climbed out and dried themselves on the grassy bank and had just time to effect a sufficient camouflage with shirts and towels before the lady appeared.

"Oh, la, la! Mais c'est fini alors messieurs? Comme ça devait être froid! Vous viendrez prendre du café chez nous?"she invited. With a typically French politeness she stayed chatting to them while they finished dressing; then carried them off to her cottage, where the coffee pot was steaming on the stove. Half a dozen glasses were produced from the cupboard in the front bedroom, the coffee was poured out, and Monsieur strengthened it with a generous dash of cognac.

"A la bonne santé, messieurs! There was a ceremonious clinking of glasses, and the honoured guests helped each other out in vigorous conversation. Madame showed them all the portrait of her son who had been "decoré à Verdun," and was now comfortably in hospital in the Midi. Old Monsieur talked of the fishing in the stream, and produced a packet of flies which would have astonished Mr. Hardy. When they rose to leave, with a great exchange of bowing and saluting (a performance in which the officers got seriously in each other's way on the doorstep) the old Frenchman invited them to make use of his rod and tackle as long as they should stay in the village. Then with a final salute, and a "Bon jour, Madame, merci beaucoup, Monsieur," they walked back to the lines. All the horses, groomed and glossy, were contentedly munching hay from nets slung on the picketing ropes, a picture of animal happiness set in the regular lines of wagons down either side, and the neat row of 18-pounders parked behind them. In the far corner of the paddock, by the road, the officers' chargers were stabled in a barn, with the grooms sitting on the straw behind them, whistling as they burnished bits and stirrup irons into silver. Phizz sent Edwards, his groom, for some sugar lumps, and after teasing Beauty and his second mare with an empty hand, finally gave them the feed they knew well enough they would get in the end. The grooms had bought straw from the farmer and had made up luxurious beds for the horses; and as Phizz patted his mounts a good-night, he left with the added pleasure of feeling they were sharing in his luxury. Now the officers separated to go to their own billets and find slacks and clean clothes waiting for them to change into; and half an hour later they met again in the mess, to sit down to dinner with shaded lamps and a real table-cloth, and Madame's oldest bottles of Pontet-Canet, warmed to the exactly right degree. And after a luxuriously long and well-cooked meal, when the Major passed round his box of cigars (chosen and sent out by his old "guv'nor" and arrived by that afternoon's mail), there was only one thing more needed; when enter Madame to ask if they would do her the honour to take a little liqueur of the Grand Marnier; which, if the big long Capitaine would kindly reach to the top shelf of the cupboard in the corner, he would find behind the cups and saucers.

The smile of content on Phizz's face as he fell asleep that night, was still there when the Major looked in next morning to call him for an early swim.

The morning was a pleasantly busy one for Phizz, as he looked after his section in the paddock. The sun was shining on the fruit trees, drying up the gems of dew on the grass; and under conditions like that things do not go wrong - they save themselves for days of mud and gloom and desolation. The horses were in good condition, well shod, and with no sores or galls. The harness was complete, and clean and supple. The guns, which had been taken over in exchange for those left behind, were new, well-oiled and free from rust. The wagons had been greased; the miscellaneous stores were all complete, no men were sick; the signallers were cleaning up instruments and cable, and so far had reported nothing wrong. In fact C/XYZ were a good battery and now under perfect conditions, were on top of their form.

After lunch Phizz exercised the privilege of an enthusiast who had fished from the Test to the Dee, and once breakfasted at the next table to Sir Edward Grey. On his way to borrow the old Frenchman's rod, he picked up Marryat, one of his sergeants, with a long cane, a line of untwisted telephone cable, and a tin of juicy worms.

"Well, Marryat, are you going to catch your own supper?" Phizz called.

"Goin' to try, sir!" he answered with a deprecating grin.

"I'm afraid there isn't much hope. The water is low and clear, and there will be lots of men bathing up above. It is altogether the wrong time of day too, and far too sunny; but it will be so jolly just to handle a rod again." And he went on to explain the details he had learned from the Frenchman the previous evening of the whereabouts of the best pools and runs in the stream. Leaving Marryat he went on for his rod and passed a very happy afternoon in the delight of throwing a fly again, and recovering the skill of his wrist and eye. Towards tea-time he gave up and took the rod back.

"V'n avez pas du poisson, alors Monsieur? Mais ça c'est bon pour la peche, l'aprés-midi. Peut être ce soir, si vous voudrez encore?"

Phizz explained that to his regret he could not try again, and with hearty thanks left the goodnatured old fellow. At the gate he heard someone call him by name, "Mr. Thurston, sir!" It was Marryat, fishing from the bank by the bottom of the garden. Phizz went up to him, and on the bank, in an extemporised basket of large leaves, he saw a long and rakish half-pounder not perhaps bearing much family resemblance to a pink-bellied Loch Leven in May, but still undoubtedly a trout of some kind. "Did you have any luck, sir?" asked the sergeant

"No, I didn't get anything."

"Well, will you have that one, sir? I'll easy get another for myself before I stop, and I think that's a nice one."

Phizz chose between the embarrassment of returning with another man's catch, and damping the sergeant's good-fellowship. "That is very nice of you, Marryat. If you are quite sure you wouldn't prefer to keep him for the sergeants' mess, I would be delighted." So he came back to brave the banter of the others when with truthful modesty he had to explain that their first congratulations were out of place.

In the evening there was a battery concert and boxing competition in the paddock. A piano borrowed from some estaminét by the wiles of the quartermaster was mounted in state in a supply wagon. The instrumentalists of the battery "band" were grouped round it, including the leading violin, whose instrument, built up out of an empty biscuit tin, with two strings of unwound "D 3" telephone wire, seemed to our uncritical ears as sweet-toned as anything Kubelik could have handled; at least it undoubtedly was a better fiddle than the guinea contraptions which were scraped by two others of his orchestra. The audience lay on the grass in a wide circle, headed by the Major and his guest, the Colonel of the Brigade, in the dignity of two borrowed chairs. The main attraction of the evening came first - the boxing. The ring had been fixed up with great care; the posts were padded with horse blankets, the ropes taut and whitened, and the grass cut. It was the preliminary heat of a battery competition, three rounds each of strenuous, if unscientific, slogging. Everyone knew well enough that the corporal-shoeing-smith must finally win, but of the score of entries there was not a round where the men did not stick up to punishment and fight it out. But the serious business was relieved by two lighter turns. The Major and Brown were to give a two-minute exhibition spar, with the Colonel as time-keeper. To a chorus of cheers they had the gloves tied on, and with pleasant smiles began light and quick sparring. Then by some accident Brown caught the Major's cheek with a jar which bruised it. The sparring slipped rapidly down to boxing, and just before the Colonel called 'Time,' Brown stopped a rich one in the right eye, which later was the finest black eye in the battery, despite the specially juicy piece of steak which his servant got from the Q.M.S.'s stores. Roars of laughter and cheers and more laughter echoed round the field as they were sponged down and took their tunics again. It echoed anew as the men near by heard the Major and Brown in a somewhat heated argument as to who was guilty of beginning the degeneration of the sparring exhibition.

"It seemed a dashed long round, too" sighed Brown at the end of it, speaking with his handkerchief held to his eye. It was the Colonel's turn to chuckle. "Yes, my boy, you two were going so well, I didn't like to stop you; so I gave you an extra half-minute or so." The other light turn was the set comic piece of the two accepted battery comedians, appropriately painted .(heaven knows how!) as clowns. As they hit at the empty air and fell over nothing, or playfully kicked each other as it were in the fashion of our gallant Allies, George Robey might have envied the loud free laughter of the audience. Then came the concert. Good and bad songs were sung, but none so bad that it had no chorus; and for that one can forgive much and applaud even the sanitary orderly's falsetto baritone in a love ditty. At last everyone stood up to the Marseillaise, played in honour of the villagers who had come to see the fun and fringed the circle of khaki; then a more rigid attention fixed the men as the chord of 'God save the King' was struck (politeness to Allies is a part of Tommy's creed, however bashfully he performs it; but his own National Anthem is a thing apart). Finally the Major called for thanks and three cheers for the Colonel, and the hearty shouts died away to the note of the trumpeter sounding the evening water and feed.

Very soon after dinner everyone went to bed, for the brigade was marching early next morning to avoid the heat of the day. At half-past three the battery had had breakfast in the dark, harnessed up and was ready for the road. They pulled out of the paddock as the sun was rising and marched at the slow pace of a long column, with hourly halts until nine o'clock, when they pulled up in a village to rest the teams and water the horses out of buckets. They pushed on again, and by eleven o'clock had reached their new billets. Brown, who had ridden on ahead, was waiting to guide them into accommodation as good as they had left. In the same way they passed each lovely day of the next fortnight, marching or resting and luxuriating in the freshness and relaxation of both. They had passed within sight of the sea, near Abbeville, and turning regretfully inland, had yet reached even more delightful country. Their health and fitness shone in their faces as they pulled into their last village, marching past the General with an easy neatness they might well be proud of.

Then, by noon next day they reached Albert. They had come back to the war, with its smashed houses and roaring guns, its crowded roads and trudging infantry and every slope hidden under camps and horse lines as far as the eye could see. A heavy thunder shower poured down now, and by the time they had reached the old No Man's Land below Fricourt, the newly-cut roads up the hill were as slippery as ice. The leading team took the hill first, and half-way up the gun and horses slithered helplessly backwards again. Picking themselves up, they tried again, but it was the task of Sisyphus. Then with gunners hauling on the wheels with drag-ropes, each vehicle in turn somehow was got to the top and the horses found their feet again. The road which they reached on the crest was one long line of transport pulling through the mud, stumbling in and out of the shell-holes, halting for interminable minutes and sweating on again. Tired infantry and loaded ambulances lurched and crawled along in the reverse stream of traffic. A battery of howitzers in the valley on the right was shooting low over their heads. Clusters of "sausage" balloons stretched behind and away on either side, double and treble banked. On the left Phizz noticed a cellar door which some enterprising individual had outlined in rustic trellis work from the broken trees by the roadside. Above was the notice, 'Town Major, Fricourt.'

"This isn't Fricourt, surely!" he said to Gurney, who was riding with him.

"Is what, Fricourt? I don't see anything at all."

"Well, there seems to be a certain amount of broken brick about, and there are more fallen trees than there were further down. Besides, we ought to be somewhere near there now."

Gurney laughed. "Well, if this is Fricourt, or any other d——d place, I'm blanked. But that's the stuff to give the Hun!"

After four hours they had moved about four miles, but they now left the 'main road' and were on better going - a wheel track across the fields. Up on the right Phizz pointed to a more heavily blasted patch of country, with a few ridiculous black rafters sticking up out of it.

"From the map, that must have been Contalmaison."

Again Gurney laughed, and pointed to the empty field they were crossing. If that was Contalmaison, what was this then?"

"Oh, God's earth, I should say." Phizz spoke facetiously, but from another mouth the words might have been a sermon.

They were silent for some time, both looking ahead. From a hidden point some half a mile in front reddish showers of earth were shooting high up into the sky every two or three minutes.

"Those are pretty big fellows, Phizz," began Gurney again.

"Yes! Must be eight-inch at least."

"And they can't be far from the road."

"Not very."

"I wonder what the Major will do. Go round it, I expect."

"I'm afraid there's too much wire about to be able to do that."

"Will he wait, or try to gallop it?"

"If we wait, we may not get in for hours, and we are already late. If we gallop it, half the teams will get crashed going down-hill with all these holes about."

"What's the betting?" asked Gurney cryptically.

"I'll give you two to one on splinters, five to one against a direct hit."

"Right you are, at a franc a time."

An order passed down the column. "Halt! Officers to the front!" Phizz and Gurney cantered up to find the Major and Brown dismounted and sitting on a derelict German ammunition wagon. They saluted.

"We'll take this next little bit, a sub-section at a time, trotting. Each of us will take one sub., myself leading. Keep the pace steady. Watch for one of those nice little pip-squeaks arriving, and then take the chance; but steady, mind!" The Major mounted and began to walk the leading sub-section forward. The heavy sough of another arrival began to be heard. "Ter-r-rott!" and they were away towards it, even before it burst. A few heavy splinters buzzed down near the teams left halted, but apparently nothing happened to the others, who went steadily down, past the still drifting smoke, and pulled up to a walk at the bottom of the hill.

"B sub., Walk March!" called Phizz, and led slowly on. The next round came sooner than he expected and was further forward down the slope. "Trot!" he called, with some three hundred yards to go. The pace he was setting seemed very slow; what a time they were taking to reach that last burst. But the Major had insisted on steadiness. Was he overdoing it, though? Eight miles an hour it should be, and he seemed to be doing a bare five. Beauty was pulling nervously, for she knew well enough what had been happening down there. She shied! an unfortunate infantryman lay where his body had been moved off the track. There were several, seven, eight — why, there must be a score, just cleared out of the way on either side, white-faced and still.

Beauty was fretting badly, and the gun team were pressing him behind. The pace could not be fast enough, the next shell was overdue now if he could judge the time aright; he had wasted valuable seconds for the men behind. What about the rear wagon? Should he canter now and make sure of it? . . . . . The gun-leaders were hard on Beauty's heels. "Steady there!" he called, and checked the pace, for he realised then that he had got so fast that the teams were getting out of hand. But it seemed like ten minutes since he started. Well, at any rate they were near the bottom now, and still the next round had not come. He raised his hand as a signal and gradually pulled up to walking pace.

"You must teach your gun team to keep their distance, Mr. Thurston. They were on your heels in a canter at one time," the Major called as Phizz passed him halted by the side of the road.

"Yes, sir !" and Phizz felt that holidays were all very well in their way, but they had a bad way of making one 'windy' at first on coming back to things. What a priceless ass he had nearly made of himself! Still, their shelling nerves would soon all be tuned up again, so that was all right. Gurney trotted up by his side, having arrived with his sub-section.

"Those deaders were a bit nasty, Phizz. It looked as if a shell had caught a whole platoon of them. Didn't it make you feel pretty windy as you went past?"

"Rather!" The major cantered past to the head of the battery and called out to them, "All O.K., water-cart and everything."

"Bon!" said Gurney; "now how much do you owe me?"

On the way up the opposite slope the battery went by an old enemy position. They looked with critical but admiring eyes at the well-planned and heavily concreted pits, built with a lavishness of labour and material which any British battery might have envied. "I wonder how the place we are going to will compare with that," Phizz muttered. They were soon to know, for the call passed down the column once more, "Officers to the front!" They cantered up, and then the Major trotted on ahead with them and the Brigade guide. He pointed out a deep and sound trench which had been built in the advance and left behind again. In front of it were four heaps of newly-filled sandbags evenly spaced, where another battery had begun to build a position and left their work unfinished.

"We must get men up to find timber for bridging the trench, and then the guns can be dropped into position just in front of it, beside the places where work has begun. The ammunition will be dumped alongside for the present, and then you, Brown, can take away all the teams at once. The men's cookhouse can be set up on the right, our mess and the signal dugout in the trench on the left. We will keep the water cart and mess cart as they are. Now will you carry on, please?"

His instructions were soon carried out, and the wagons and limbers and teams were all got away.

The servants were getting tea ready, the men's cooks were boiling dixies, the men attending to their guns and equipment, the officers looking round at the possibilities of the position and searching for any available dugouts or accommodation ready-made. The Major had announced that immediately after tea they must begin to dig in, and Phizz and Gurney had to plan their scheme of work. The Major himself was arranging the aiming posts for the guns when an orderly appeared at the position and delivered a message to him.

He swore, not loud but very deep, and called for Thurston.

"I say, Phizz, here's a bit of a bombshell. Brigade have sent for you to report there at once."

"Do they say what for?"

"No, but one wouldn't need to guess twice," the Major answered, handing him the pink slip. "You had better take your things prepared for going up to infantry; it may save you having to walk back here. But stay and have tea first."

"The message says 'at once ; urgent!" Phizz said rather sadly, "and you will have signed the receipt and timed it."

"Oh, that's all right. It isn't a bit of use knocking yourself up at the beginning of a job if it really is urgent. One moment, and I'll come along with you to see what the servants have raised in the way of tea."

"Right-ho, Major. I'll get my stuff out of my kit, so as to be ready."

The mess cook was a man with no imagination and no ability in cooking, yet kept his job by never failing at a time of difficulty. Bread and butter, jam and paste and cake, and above all, hot fresh tea were ready. Though only the cups and one knife had been as yet unearthed from the mess crockery, that did not matter to anyone as hungry as the Major and his subalterns; they sat on the edge of the trench and passed. the knife round with the food, and the good humour of the picnic was perhaps helped by the unusual difficulties of partaking of it. After it Phizz got up somewhat reluctantly at the prospect of a very long evening's work waiting for him, and filled his cigarette case from Gurney's, his own stock not having been found yet. Then he took up the haversack which his servant had brought, and slung it on his shoulder.

"I *shall* be annoyed if I find I am coming back again, and don't need this stuff. Well, so long, and work hard; I shall expect to come back to a dugout as safe as a house, and as comfortable." Phizz trudged off alone, in the direction of the Brigade headquarters' map reference.

Now some of the peculiarities of that delightful invention, the map-reference, have already been mentioned. But on the Somme battlefield, where every house and village had disappeared, where old roads had been overgrown and new roads had been worn across the fields, and, moreover, the area behind the old trench system, even as it had been before the battle, was badly mapped, then hunting for anything was apt to prove a little complicated. But the place which he was now setting out to find was an old German dugout, entirely hidden below ground, and all the earth from inside it had been carried away by its methodical constructors; so for Phizz, dragging over the sticky clay fields, still wet from the afternoon showers, the odds were pretty slender. After drawing blank at the first point he tried, he put his map away as useless, and tackled the problem in the Sherlock Holmes spirit, which brought him to an infantry brigade headquarters instead of the one he wanted. However, a Good Samaritan of a Brigade Major, wearing a ribbon that brought Phizz to a smarter salute than any amount of gold and red tabs would have done, took him along to the place he was searching for, half a mile away.

Phizz explained to the Colonel on his arrival that he was late through having been lost.

"Major Osborne should have kept the messenger as a guide for you, of course. As it is, I am afraid you may yet get caught by dark on your way up to the line, and I have no guide who knows the way. Now, I am sorry to have had to take you, especially as Osborne is short-officered already. But these next four days are going to be extremely important, and it is essential to have an experienced officer who is good at reading his map."

Phizz looked up to see if for once in his life the Colonel was trying to be humorous, but his face showed no flicker, and presumably he had no thought of the recent exhibition of how to get lost by map.

The Colonel went on: "Now the date and objectives of the main attack, I can't give you; but it will be immediately preceded by a minor attack on the Sedan redoubt. The battalion of the Rifles at present in the line is being kept in for that, and will then be relieved at once by one of our own battalions. You will be my liaison officer with the battalion in both shows, but your most important work will be this: we have put in an advanced enfilading gun a mile to the north, screened by Square Wood, but only five hundred yards from the front line. The Sedan redoubt is too close to our own trenches for effective bombardment by heavies to be really practicable, and this enfilade gun will have to prepare it for the assault. That must be done absolutely thoroughly. The redoubt has cost us two useless attacks so far, and this time, for the success of the big attack it is essential to have it and hold it. You understand?"

"Yes, sir. And about telephonists and lines?"

"The Adjutant will explain that to you. 'B' battery is providing the men, and you will take over from the officer of the old division who is now there. Well, that is all for the present, but I will try to get up and see you before the big day. Be careful of yourself, for remember, any hitch may cost a lot.

Good luck, Thurston." He stood up and shook Phizz's hand.

This unusual ceremony made Phizz smile drily to himself. "The hearty old pessimist thinks I'm a goner this trip," he thought; "dirty work waiting at the cross-roads, and he says 'put all you know into the job,' and then 'be careful.' His blood tingled as he thought of the splendid shooting which seemed to be promised; with only himself to worry about, and none of his own men, the thought of danger could be put right away and forgotten. But he had one thing to ask.

"The big day, sir: is it to be the break-through at last?"

"God knows, my boy. I have not been told . . . . but this road above was labelled this afternoon, 'Cavalry Track, C.' "

"Good! We guessed the division wouldn't be here for nothing."

"Yes, Thurston, I believe we shall have Fritz this time. But you must hurry away now." He turned to the Adjutant: "Give him the instructions about communications and send for the men to go with him."

This was soon done, and collecting coat and haversack and maps, he climbed out of the dugout. A reiterated chorus of good wishes followed him, whose unusual heartiness was 'enough to give the men shellshock on the spot,' according to his own light-hearted description of it afterwards.

He asked the men their names as they walked along, and chatted about the war to learn what experience they had had, and how keen they were. To his surprise each of the three seemed a thoroughly good man, and it impressed him more than anything else with the importance of the Sedan redoubt; for an adjutant does not get really good men out of a battery without much troublesome insistence. Satisfied with their good humour, he prepared them for the difficulty there would be about finding the battalion headquarters.

The Corporal laughed. "They say, sir, that Fritz doesn't do much firing on the trenches by day, but keeps it all for the support line and communication trenches at night time. You said headquarters would be at the corner of the support line and the big communication trench, sir?"

"That's it, corporal. We have to find where the Boche is shelling heaviest, and go straight for it — I don't think!"

It was now dark enough for them to be glad of the bright flickering Very lights which were continually shooting up from the front line, stretching right round the salient and seeming almost to close in behind them. The going was very bad, for the track wound in and out round the lips of shell-hole touching shell-hole. Our own guns were reasonably quiet for a battle front, but yet occasionally bright blinding flashes blazed around them, and the shock of it would at times make them wince. They minded this far more than the fairly liberal sprinkling of shells which echoed in the night air: that is nothing to compare with the feeling that the next gun which shoots low over your head will finish the work of cutting right through both ear-drums. Almost every part of the valley slope seemed to be a gun position, and it was with great relief that the little party got out in front of the battery area and into that pleasant oasis of the trench system between the guns and the infantry support lines; for in this zone, if one keeps away from the infantry transport roads, such as they may be, there is practically nothing for the enemy to waste his shells on. Ahead was a heavy harassing barrage, clearly heard, but only seen when the Very lights rose up; and now that the dangerous hour after dusk was over these were less frequent than they had been. Phizz, leading the way, fell over a trench board, and found that it was part of a track.

"I think we might try this one, corporal. It is leading somewhere in the right direction," said Phizz, and wound up in a prodigious yawn.

"Tired, sir?"

"Fairly. We left Hericogne early this morning, and I have been riding or walking ever since."

"Let me carry your haversack, sir. I am not carrying much." As the corporal had his own kit, and four days' rations and a telephone, a coil of cable and part of a wireless "earth buzzer" slung all round him, Phizz would have had to hang the haversack round the man's neck himself, so he thanked him for something that showed the right spirit even if it were not quite what one would call a firm offer.

The duckboards had been somewhat knocked about by shells. Some were there, some weren't. Of those which were, a certain number jumped up as Phizz trod on one end, or slid over as he reached the other. Even allowing for the accepted eccentricities of wooden tracks as laid by gentlemen who rely on never having to use them, and as subsequently rearranged by the uninvited interference of obstreperous enemy battery commanders, yet he had just made up his mind that this particular one was really beyond the usable limit, when in front he heard a quiet hum of automatic and unemphasised blasphemy.

"Some infantry ahead, sir," said the corporal, peering past him; "a carrying party, I should say, by the sound of them."

"Yes," Phizz agreed, "their language is a bit —— Damn!" as he stumbled into a wet hole through looking at them. He walked on again, trying to push up past the side of the carrying party to reach the officer in charge. Trench revetment material was being carried, and the men were loaded with sheets of corrugated iron or "expanded metal" or the big wooden frames which are just not so awkwardly designed for carrying as to be impossible. The party shuffled on very slowly in the dark, feeling the way carefully where a man in front had tripped up or caught his load on a low hanging line of cable. These men of the Somme battle, by the time their division was nearly exhausted and on the point of being pulled out, were vastly different from the clean alert soldiers whom Phizz knew on "peace" fronts. The smell of mud and toil and unwashed weariness hung round them, the odour of the life they were living and the death which lurked around. They were a long party, and before Phizz could pass by half of them, the track ran into the narrowness of a communication trench, and with his men he was sandwiched into the party.

He spoke to the man ahead of him. "Do you happen to know if this leads to battalion headquarters of the Rifles?" There was no answer. He touched the man, who woke to comprehension with a startled jerk.

"No, sir, I don't, I'm sure."

"Do you know where you are going or where you are now?"

"No, I don't, sir. Th' officer knows."

"What are you?" "D Company."

"What of?"

"The Rifles, sir."

"Oh, you *are* the Rifles, then. That is splendid," said Phizz. "You have no idea where you are going with these things?"

"No, sir, th' officer knows."

The party stopped its shuffling forward. Men eased themselves of their loads, then almost at once had to pick them up again to stumble on a few more steps, then cushion into the men ahead and pull up again with an oath. The same thing kept on, and it was clear that the trench was blocked by something in front. So after several exasperating minutes of this, Phizz clambered up out of the trench, gave a hand to the corporal and the others, and they tried to make their way along the top. It was a hard business, from the irregularity of the parapet and the shell-holes, helped by the dumping everywhere along it of dropped material and coils of wire. But in the way which one soon learns in a school where pitfalls and discomforts are only incidents in a quick life, Phizz was not even conscious of the nightmare difficulties as anything to worry about in themselves. They made the journey longer, it would be longer before they found the end, take longer to get clear through shelling, that was all.

In this way they passed along the parapet until a certain nosiness made Phizz stop to see if this was the head of the block. A company going out to reserve had jammed in the narrow trench with the carrying party, and now were trying to squeeze past. Phizz called down his enquiry about headquarters, and an officer below answered: "Go up here to O.G.I., then to the right down Murray Walk, till you reach the old road."

"How far is it to O.G.I., please?"

"Oh, about four hundred yards; up there where he is shelling. There, now, you see that crump burst; well, that's about it."

A sergeant of the company which was squeezing by so slowly took up the tale. "Aye, that's it. He got three of our platoon there, an' two more wounded. You'll find them there on this side, and the old trench there running out of this one is O.G.I. And they aren't 'alf givin' it fair 'ell, neither."

"I shouldn't stay up there if I were you," the officer spoke again; "he machine-guns at night, straight down from somewhere on the ridge. Just then a shell whined grimly down and burst softly some few score yards down the trench. Phizz picked himself up and thanked the infantryman, but preferred to push across the open where a machine-gun might sweep, rather than stay where there certainly was shelling. He left the trench with its block of men squeezing and swearing, or dozing and waiting, too weary to be interested even in the next shell.

Now Phizz saw quite clearly that the Boche had a pretty dense night barrage stretching all the way along the support area, and snatching down each communication trench from moment to moment. If he could make out the old road when he reached it, he might cut straight forward through the barrage, and either go down the road itself or find any trench which would circle round to it again. That was at any rate better than making one of the hopeless block in a trench marked out for barrage.

"Thank heaven we aren't infanteers, having to keep down in that trench block for hours waiting to be scuppered any minute," said Phizz.

"But why don't they get out, sir, like us?" asked the corporal.

"Well, there are more of them, and so it's more risky; then there would be more chance of a party getting lost, or out of touch, or ——"

Crack, *crack crack* CRACK, CRACK, crack .... the sharp note of a machine-gun keyed up as it swept towards and over them, then dropped as it passed.

"——In short," continued Phizz, "that is why!" and the little party got up from the shell-holes into which they had hastily ducked, and went on again with a wary eye always on the next hole ahead. But the belt they were crossing now was, moreover, the fringe of the barrage area. There was a hardly explicable impression as if the long belt of bursting shells echoing in one continuous roar, began to thin out as they closed into it and concentrated their minds more and more on their own immediate bit, their ears keenly tuned to select from the general noise the note of any which came towards them. From a distance the belt of death seemed too dense for anything to pass it, yet in going through it was just a shell here, another there, quickly enough to keep them vividly alert, near enough for the splinters to zip and splash around them; but making straight forward, jumping over a dozen shallow trenches fallen into disuse or never completed, they soon got through to the lighter fringe of chance splinters and short shrapnel bursts. Here they stopped to ask the way from some machinegunners, firing over the top of a trench through a sack to hide the flashes. They directed Phizz back into the middle of the barrage, along a trench which was the very heart of it. Stumbling along this as low under the broken parapet as they could go, past a few sentries crouching like themselves, over the legs of men snuggled asleep in holes scraped out of the trench walls, through the choking smell which hangs over new shell-holes - at last they came to a fairly well made bit of track, with a gas-gong at the corner seen in the opportune flicker of a rocket light. Phizz found some dugout steps near by, screened by a blanket. The stairway was blocked with men sleeping on the bare muddy steps, sprawled over each other for warmth. The air inside was bad and heavy, colder even than the night air outside, a combination of qualities that might have made a Sarah Gamp stop and think.

Phizz climbed down over the men as carefully as he could, but yet disturbed some, who only rolled stiffly back again. At the bottom he came into a twenty-foot long tunnel; in one corner a greasy cook was frying a steak over a noisy Primus stove; officers and men were sitting down on their coats, or on the bare floor; two or three candles lit up the reek of the atmosphere. An elderly man, grey haired and unshaven, sitting in a stained trench coat on the only chair in the tunnel, glared at Phizz.

"Go back and come down the right way. What do you mean by disturbing my orderlies like that?" Astounded, Phizz began to explain who he was. Another half-bearded man rose from the far end of the dugout, and as the old man cut Phizz short, beckoned to him to go, and himself stepped up the corresponding stairway at his end. Angry, but realising that this was no time for having any personal feelings at all, Phizz went back over the sleepers again and met the man he was to relieve, waiting for him at the top. He led him round to the head of a similar stairway, with men also sleeping on it from top to bottom, but a sort of clear way down between them.

"You are my relief, of course. That was Colonel Campbell, but the poor old boy is nearly done in; out of all his officers he has eight left, he has lost most of his men, and to-day he has been strafed for the condition of the defences and also told he has to stay in for another attack on the Sedan. Well, are you all right?"

"Yes, thanks. So sorry to be late, of course. Where is your telephone dugout?"

The other gunner laughed. "This and one other are the only dugouts in the sector. The other has two company headquarters in it, and is worse than this. The Boche knows them both, and shells us all night, and then all day. But in here is where we fix up. My fellows will show yours the line, but it is "dis" at present and you won't be able to mend it; any urgent calls you can get through on the infantry brigade line, which is still working. My O.P. was in the front line, but you can't see anything from it; anyone will show you it in the morning, and I'll get off at once if you don't mind. We are going back to rest to-morrow, thank God!"

Phizz was not much impressed by the gentleman's keenness, but took the situation as inevitable. He and his men would have to be up by dawn to work on the line, but meanwhile they could do no good in the dark. Supper seemed out of the question, and even breakfast pretty problematical for himself, who had relied on the hospitality of the battalion. However, for the moment the thing to do was clearly to join the sleepers below. The men dropped all their equipment in the place cleared by the outgoing signallers, with a sigh of pleased relief at having arrived here at last. Phizz went down to take the part of the floor which his predecessor had left him.

"How long have you been in France, Gunner?" asked the Colonel with a very slight moderation of his surliness.

"Six months longer than your battalion, sir," Phizz replied crisply as he took off his trench coat to lie down on.

"And when did you get that?" Colonel Campbell pointed to the strip of ribbon on Phizz's tunic, which he now caught sight of.

"Loos!" The name was sufficient date." Mmph. Have you had any supper?"

"I have not."

"Well, you won't get much, but we can give you some steak, I expect. Hardy," he called to the cook, "give this officer anything you can get him . . . . By the way, what is your name?"

"Thurston, sir."

"Right. That is the Adjutant, sleeping next to the biscuit box"; - that officer turned uneasily as he was mentioned, but remained asleep. The Colonel continued, "The second-in-command is out at the burial place. That is all of us."

While Phizz ate a scrap meal, sitting on the floor, the Colonel eased his worries by telling of some of the costly adventures the battalion had had in their long spell of the battle; but as soon as Phizz had done, he recommended him to sleep while he could. Phizz wrapped his coat round himself and was soon unconscious of the heavy thuds above which shook earth down from the roof, or the cold dank draught which spread down from the stairways. But it was a very tired sleep, broken into by others stepping over him, scraps of conversation, or the next man to himself turning stiffly over. He seemed to have just dozed for half an hour when his shoulder was shaken.

"It is getting light, sir !" It was the corporal waking him for the day's work. He sat up.

"Would you like a cup of tea?" The cook had come along with a big enamel mug steaming fragrantly.

Phizz thanked him through a stifled yawn, and began to feel for the flask in his pocket.

"There is some rum in it, sir, it is the same as I gets ready for the Colonel going out at Stand to. He's been gone a-piece now, but I kept it 'ot."

§

Now Phizz's work for the next three days covers for the author as a fellow-gunner almost the most interesting part of his share in the battle of the Somme. But the reader might be wearied by the details of his many difficulties in maintaining telephone communication, and discovering a really suitable post from which to observe the redoubt; how at last from a just accessible shell-hole in front of our trenches he had three days of wonderfully satisfactory shooting with the Lone Gun most admirably sited, firing so accurately at its short range that he could do anything he liked with it, and sweeping so effectively right down the Hun trench that it soon drove the garrison into the shelter of their dugouts and left the trench itself almost unmanned; how sniping with the gun or with a borrowed rifle he got more than one Hun who tried to dash past the gaps he had cleared in the parapet, and how the enemy deluged Square Wood with shells and trench mortars in an attempt to silence the gun, leaving only one corner untouched - the corner where the gun was so well hidden. On the night preceding the attack on the redoubt, he kept the gun firing sudden bursts down the trench, which stopped all attempts at repair work in the dark, and next morning he slept in the bottom of an old trench, where he was out of the way of traffic passing over him. He was waked about mid-day by an orderly bringing him his copy of the operation orders for the minor attack of that evening and the greater battle of the following dawn.

All day, along the whole battle front, a very heavy destructive barrage had been working on the enemy support lines, his batteries, and all his communications. The Hun was lying fairly low himself, saving up for his concentrated counter-preparation at night. Over lunch Phizz arranged with the Colonel to have a final harassing shoot all the way down the Sedan redoubt, and then to leave it in peace until the concentrated attack barrage was to open, three minutes before the men went over the top. Phizz crawled out to his O.P. and did this satisfactorily, and returned to headquarters for an early tea in the hour that remained to him. Then he went back to his predecessor's old observation post in the front line itself. Everywhere around the Salient the heavy firing was continued, but over the redoubt was a suspicious lull before the evening storm. The front line was packed close with every available man pushed in for the battalion's last desperate fling, and sadly depleted as it was, still there was a man nearly to each yard of trench, and another battalion was taking the flank of the attack.

So this little team in khaki stood waiting for the starting gun. It is the finest of all sports, the greatest game of all that they had to play, and whatever share the fields of Eton may have had in any winning of it, that same share must be credited to the back alleys and cinder patches, the parks and the recreation grounds which had been the nursery of most of those who stood together in that forward line, picked to play for England. How closely parallel it was to those other, less vital games that they had played - the same reward, a piece of ribbon instead of a club cap or a blue scarf perhaps, but still the same thing; the same inconclusiveness, with many another match to be played before the final victory was settled, yet always the supreme importance of winning this present point now; the same interest afterwards in looking through the newspaper to see if its accounts did justice to our game, only so often to find a bare note of the result, or no mention of it at all; the same tense "needle" while waiting and shivering through ghastly minutes between being ready and the word Go! Of course, if you push the parallel too far, you may find the discrepancy in thinking of the penalties, of the price to be paid for missing the goal. But that, thank God, a man does not think about; Hope wears a bandage round her eyes, and seldom before the harp has clattered down from her final pluck at the string does that last one snap. Occasionally one may have seen it go, and then one leaves that scene aside, and tells no man; leaves it to best-selling novelists and minor poets.

Phizz watched the man on either side of him, and thought of the crew of the first "Torpid" he had coached at Oxford in the Spring before the War. The picture came back to his mind as he had watched the boat at the starting punt, from the bang of the five-minute gun. He saw them again fidgeting with their oars in the rowlocks, smiling wanly at some feeble banter, answering in hoarsely broken short sentences which they probably thought were not different from their speaking voices; then a welcome respite as a box of resin was passed down the boat, and for a few seconds gave them something to occupy their hands with: the bang of the minute gun two seconds before it was due: the frenzied checking of stop-watches, calmed by a quiet reassurance from an older hand: the taut activity as the old boatman pushed out their craft to the end of the coxswain's bung: the rigid nervous adjustments and tension as the final seconds began to race on to the zero: eight, seven, six . . . .

Yes, it was just what he was watching now. Few of the men in the trench had experience: true, some of them were hardened veterans of three devastating weeks of the Somme, but every detail the battalion could scrape together had been pushed in for this last fling, from the transport lines, from the band, from the sick bay, cooks, orderlies, specialists, down to the last draft from the base arrived in the nick of time and shoved forward before their khaki had lost its tell-tale freshness. They stood beside their rifles, bayonets fixed; bantered each other as they shivered a little; made their tension the more marked as they forced the mask of unconcern. What was noticeable was only to be seen in the tiny details, just glinting from the drab casualness of every-day monotony. One man moved a letter from one breast pocket to another. An eagle-eyed sergeant was on to him sharply, for by some queer confusion of ideas, the carrying of letters had been forbidden (an order more usual for raiders, going over without regimental badges or identity marks). The culprit sniggered like a schoolboy caught cribbing, and trampled the letter in the glutinous brown mud. Some buckets of bombs were passed down, and this seemed to ease the strain. An officer came along, checking the placing of the scaling ladders. Phizz had met him before, and they chatted for a time: he described the officers of the relieving battalion who had come up that morning to look at the line they were to take over, and Phizz tried to recall the names of these people from his own division, and to fit a name to each personal description as if their identity were a thing that really mattered. He was beginning to feel anxious about the results of his shooting on the front of the Sedan, and his attempts to break gaps in the wire entanglement that had hedged it, but neither of them mentioned it. An N.C.O. came up with a rum-jar, and suggestively tinkled an enamelled mug against the side. The infantryman compared the setting of his watch with the two stop-watches which Phizz had brought with him, and they argued anxiously about the few seconds' discrepancy they showed.

"Beg pardon, sir," the man with the mug interrupted, "there isn't much time left for the rum, sir." His officer took the hint, and gave the first mugfull to Phizz. As he drank to "the best of luck," a swift picture of that tangled hedge of wire crossed his mind, and his toast was deep. Then the cup was passed along, and men took as much as they could, once, without a choke. It may be imagination, but again it may not, that no rum can ever be so heartening as that which was sent up to the front line before the zero hour. So the cup was filled again and the officer went down with it into the next bay. The old strain reasserted itself. Ten minutes to go, and how slowly they went. How isolated was their little bit of life, boxed in that hole in the clay, guns everywhere behind them seeming to hammer everywhere except at the patch of Germany which lay so few yards ahead, neighbours on either flank only concerned with their own little stretch, and barely casually interested in what was to happen so close to them. Yet it was vitally important; and would it even have a line in to-morrow's communiqué? Perhaps not, not big enough for that, and yet to this little batch of men, ignorant - are not most of us still wondering? - of why it had to be, it meant just everything. Oh, hang this morbid seriousness! Think of Piccadilly, or the crowd just leaving the matinees for tea at the Waldorf or wherever it might be. No, thoughts like that only make it worse. Hurrah, here comes the infantry subaltern again, someone to talk to. They compared watches once again, and he had passed on. Another long minute, and one of the men sat down on the fire-step, gazing at the brown trench wall with his head in his hands.

"Get up there, you ——!" the sergeant swore at him. "Sit down afterwards you can if you like, and maybe Jerry will help you with one in your blank guts." The unfortunate soldier, one of the recruit draft, stood up with a jerk, his face drawn into a half-sheepish grin, half-resentful sneer, as he picked up his rifle. "There you go again," burst out the sergeant once more, as the bayonet tip was brought up above the parapet line, "that's right, go over and tell 'em we're coming, I would if I was you, you silly-faced son of ——."

Should he butt into this abuse, Phizz wondered, and try to hearten the man more tactfully. But the infantry were beginning to hitch at their equipment, handle their shovels, or take up their rifles. He looked at his watch; good heavens, only half a minute before the barrage should begin. And the seconds were going fast now, simply racing round and heart beating hard: would it be all right? Twelve, eleven, ten, eight, six . . . .

Bang! a single premature round screamed past. Bang, bang, others raggedly pursued it. Then he stopped thinking, as time and place were closed down on by a tornado of hurtling crashes. Beneath the sudden overwhelming monstrosity of it he huddled forward, cringing against the trench wall. Then a blaze, and a body-rending crash, and the blindness of encircling smoke; and when he could see again, at his feet there was a white foot, stripped (by some freak of explosion) of boot and sock and puttees, and blown along the trench without a spot of blood on the visible surface of it. The sharp criss-cross rattle of close-range machine-guns broke into his ears with an acuteness that told its own tale. Smashed at the start by shell-fire, pinned down to the trench by that raking hail of bullets - it was failure-yes and what else? Again that smashing explosion, just to his right, and splinters had brought down all four men between him and the burst, but their bodies had just been enough to shield him. Through the smoke he saw a khaki figure on the parapet of the next bay. Yet none of the men near him had set out. Well, it was not his job to lead them, but to go over with the second wave. But would there be a second wave at all? His own pay was ten shillings and sixpence a day, and for these men a paltry shilling. (He could laugh afterwards at the ludicrous inconsequence of his thoughts then, yet so they ran in their bare simplicity.) Anyway, better try and scramble forward through the bullets, it could not be as bad as waiting for the next of those ghastly explosions to pitch on top of him, and blast him into nothingness. Yes, he would make a show of earning his half-guinea, Here goes I and he sprawled forward over the parapet. Someone walked up to him and gave him a hand.

"Come along, men, you must get across now." It was not Phizz who spoke, but the khaki figure that had come along the front of the parapet. The machine-gunning was irritatingly close, but was passing over their heads, and was our own machine-gun barrage. Except for an occasional stray shrapnel burst, No Man's Land was a "healthy" oasis between our shelling, which had lifted back to the support lines, and the enemy S.O.S. barrage which was going too "safe," too far back, to be serious. Khaki-clad soldiers were picking their way through the enemy wire ahead, everywhere excepting just opposite where Phizz now stood. He recognised in the man who had helped him the captain of this company, passing down his line to see that all his first wave men were making good.

"Hallo! I thought the whole front line had been blown to hell," Phizz stammered somewhat sheepishly in the reaction of the placid reality compared with the battle, murder and sudden death he had keyed himself up to; "at any rate, all of us here, except me, have got it in the neck."

"Yes, I saw two of our 'toffee-apples' drop short," the infantryman answered, "and a dickens of a mess they make, wherever they drop. But you'd better get across if you are going; see you later. Good luck, Gunner." Phizz walked across to one of the gaps in the battered tangle of wire that he had himself cleared in the previous days of shooting. On his flanks men of the second wave were clambering out of the trench, and picking their way across the waste of shell-holes. Some of them drifted across to the gap through which he led the way, and they dropped into an apparently empty bay of the German front trench. At the far end of it from Phizz there was a battered bit of concrete showing through the shell-scattered sand-bagging.

"'Ere, stop that, curse yer," a man shouted. Phizz looked and saw him stooping to the entrance of a dugout shaft beneath the concrete roofing, poised with a bomb in his drawn-back hand. "Down it, I tell yer:—all right, then," he added, and threw, and drew aside from the mouth of the shaft to wait for the explosion.

"A Hun down there, telephoning," he explained to his mates. For a long three seconds nothing happened: then a soft muffled burst, and some greywhite smoke wisps blew out of the dugout. Phizz edged along to it.

"Look out, sir, there's a Fritz down there," the man warned him, and tossed another couple of bombs down, to make more sure of his fate. "He was signalling, and wouldn't stop."

Phizz noticed a telephone cable leading up the trench, but a shell had cut it a few yards further along, so that whatever the message this enemy had given his life to try to send, he must have called to the other end in vain.

A thought of the courage of that vainly gallant sacrifice passed quickly through Phizz's mind. But this was no time to think about things. He worked his way round the bend into the next bay.

"Ah, good evening, how are you?" someone greeted him warmly.

"Good evening," he answered in automatic reply to the greeting, in the instant before his mind had grasped the fact that the man was a Boche; " ——eh, blank your eyes," he continued, bringing up his revolver.

"I am Kamerad, and you will protect, Mister Lieutenant," the German whined, as he lifted his arms into that ridiculous attitude of terrified surrender which only a middle-aged German in the ugliness of a tight field-grey uniform could achieve; and clumsily backing in his terror, he collapsed over a fallen body in the bottom of the trench. Behind him crouched a smaller, but still more pot-bellied reservist, who as soon as he too was exposed to view clapped his hand to the little trickle of blood from the tiniest of splinter wounds above his right eye, and bellowed in an agony of petition for protection, while in his left hand he held out his red-ringed cap as though in ludicrous offer of it in return for his life.

Phizz was getting rather anxious about his own single-handed position in this bay. Over the top of the parapet he could see other Germans scurrying (like frightened ponies, funking a jump but more afraid of the spur if they refuse) across to No Man's Land, eyes darting from one part of the line to another in mortal terror that they would be shot at before reaching the haven of our old front line, tripping into shell-holes through not looking instead where they were going, and lying squirming there on their bellies with arms still feebly waving over the backs of their heads in token of "Kameraad!" He signalled to these others to follow them, but at that instant one of the Rifles appeared at the top end of the bay, his bayonet red, his eyes reflecting its redness.

"Who are you?" he shouted out, his voice hoarse with the drunkenness of blood.

"Steady, man," Phizz answered; "you can see I am an officer-artillery: these are prisoners."

"Damn all prisoners," the man shouted back, "I'd stick the lot of the ——." But a sergeant and more men came along behind him, exuberant at the ease with which the line had fallen, but clear-headed, and fighting clean. Phizz left the situation to them, and pushed on to follow a communication trench up to the real objective, the second line which backed the salient front of the old redoubt. At the north end, there was the active passing-up of bombs and barbed wire, and filling up of the trench-block to protect this flank; nothing but this and a few bodies, and that inexplicable characteristic smell of Hun trench, would have betrayed the fact that it was not a solid part of our front system. A corporal sat at the corner of the communication trench squatting on an enemy machine-gun as he yarned to two of the barbed wire carriers about his capture of it.

"Yus," he said, "them in the front line was hands up 'afore ever we got within yards of them, what few was left, and that wasn't many. We was over here in no time; the 'barridge' hadn't lifted as yet. Some of these fellows did a bit of fighting, throwing them piffling little egg-bombs as we got close, and then surrendering as soon as they had thrown them: all but these 'ere machine-gunners: they was just beginning to get nasty when their gun jammed, and me and Bill Pocock was on to 'em then like knife, we was....." His chatter went on, but Phizz had to get along to the other end, where a harder fight had been fought. His way was hampered by the condition to which bombardment had reduced the trench, and the work going on to clear it and fix up some sort of parapet on the side facing the Hun. A couple of men with buckets of bombs walked past along the outside of the trench between the old parapet and its protecting entanglement. Phizz got out and followed them, and had nearly caught them up when the leading man collapsed with a soft groan, bleeding from a neat bullet hole in the temple. Ducking into the shelter of the parapet, Phizz just caught sight of a rifle barrel foolishly lifted in the air as the German sniper drew it back for reloading. Peeping cautiously round a shell-hole gap in the parapet, he saw the tops of two grey-green steel helmets moving slightly as their wearers moved about in the concealment of a large shell-hole some eighty yards away. He reached out for the dead man's rifle and with slow care laid it across the parapet, then peeped again from a few yards away. The helmets still showed, and no rifle. He went back to his own rifle, and perhaps in too nervous haste, fired, and missed.

"Blahst yer," an angry voice called from the concealment of the trench, "what the —— do you mean by shooting past a bloke like that, yer ruddy idiot: nearly through my blinking earhole, blank yer."

"Sorry," Phizz apologised, across the hole in the parapet. "There are two Hun snipers with their heads exposed, and I've just missed them. I'm not much of a marksman myself. Would you like to try?"

"Catch me!" the other answered promptly, and went on with his digging in the bottom of the trench.

"Well, look out, then," Phizz answered him, "I'll get one for one somehow, if it takes me till dark."

"Aye, if he don't get you first," was the encouraging retort as the infantryman sat down to watch from one side of the gap, apparently more disgruntled at being interrupted in his bit of work than interested in the duel with the enemy. But Phizz persuaded him to draw the Hun's attention with his "tin hat" above the trench line. Crack! it drew a shot, and instantaneously Phizz raised himself to the sights of the rifle he had left on the parapet. Again the Hun was incautiously drawing back his rifle, with his whole face exposed. Phizz fired: there was an impression of a black splodge beneath the low peak of the helmet, and the rifle barrel jerked sharply upwards. Honour was satisfied. He did not mind about the second man. But even as he crawled on, crouched well under cover, a chance short round of our artillery barrage dropped close by where he had been shooting, and looking towards the smoke of it, over the top he saw a German leap up and dash for the rear. A long three seconds passed, and even as the enemy dropped to cover again, half a dozen rifles cracked and kicked up scattered spurts of dust about his feet or beyond him, but left him untouched. Again he leapt up, and more rifles shot at him, mixed with the staccato rattle of a Lewis gun, yet apparently unharmed he dropped (almost, it seemed, slowly) into a concealed trench, and that was the last glimpse Phizz was to have of an enemy that day. At the extreme south end of the objective he could just make out a block in the trench, with occasional "potato-masher" bombs lobbed from the far side, all dropping short of a little group in khaki who replied from time to time by bowling a Mills bomb across the barrier with the leisured action of a slow high cricket lob. There was nothing else to see.

Phizz had now to hasten back and report the position, and try to get into touch with his Lone Gun that it might fire down the trench beyond that bombing block, in defence against whatever counter-attack preparations might be hidden there. Making his way back down a convenient fold in the contours of the low ridge which the Sedan redoubt had occupied, he crossed the old No Man's Land over the open. A party of pioneers were digging alongside a zig-zag line of dirty tape laid to mark out a new communication trench. They were working hard, but certainly not in any frenzied hurry, occasionally pausing to spit on their hard palms, and mumble something about the snarling shrapnel bursts which were beginning to splash more frequently about the front of the old redoubt. Other men were plodding across, lugging heavy boxes of rifle ammunition, or awkward loads of trench material, their eyes intent on their destination and the best way to it. In contrast with these were men returning more or less casually to our own line, towards the thicker German barrage which still concentrated mainly on our old support line. Two pairs of Huns with stretchers picked their way across, apparently untended, continually glancing back over their shoulders in an anxiety about their own countrymen's shells which they had probably seldom betrayed so transparently about their enemies'. Through this scattered traffic Phizz reached the ghastly little bay from which he had scrambled in such trepidation a short two hours earlier. The corrugated iron sheets which revetted the bottom of it still showed the clean edges of the splinter holes which riddled every inch of them. That extraordinary freak of a naked limb lay there still, but mud-soiled and partly trampled into the floor. Everything else had been cleared away; two or three new men occupied the bay, and that was all, all there was to show that those concentrated seconds of hell had not been just a nasty dream.

"Anyone seen anything of a gunner signaller about here?" asked Phizz.

"Yes, sir: there's one of · 'em somewhere down here," one of the Riflemen answered. Then stooping to a little cubby-hole burrowed out (in defiance of theory and the brass hats) from beneath the parapet, he called out, "'Ere, mate, 'ere's your bloke wants you quick!"

The telephonist scrambled out from a comfortable nest of empty sandbags, still holding the copy of "French without a master in thirty days," which had kept him interested in the middle of this monotonous adventure of the infantry around him. He straightened his hat and buttoned up his opened coat.

"Well, Milligan, what has happened to you here?" Phizz asked.

"Corporal Baker sent me here to wait for you, sir," the signaller explained. "After he got wounded he tried to mend the line, but it was no good, sir, and he came back to battalion headquarters and said he would carry on there till night time, and sent me here. All the lines are 'dis,' but I couldn't do anything by myself, and the corporal thought I'd best just wait for you here, sir."

"Right, we will go back to headquarters now," said Phizz, and they passed down the trench to join the congested streams that mingled in the narrow traffic way; ammunition men, carrying parties, runners, stretcher-bearers, prisoners, walking wounded, pioneers, and all the odds and ends of humanity that waggled in the tail of the attack. Luckily the enemy artillery fire was more ragged than usual. All along the line our own guns were hammering their bombardment in preparation for the morrow, smashing down on all the known enemy batteries as well as his transport roads and communication trenches. Belated aeroplanes were whooming overhead, watching in the last minutes of dusk for any reply the enemy might try to make.

At last they reached the battalion dugout, and found it curiously empty. and peaceful after the hectic crowding in the trench above. The Colonel was sitting on his solitary chair, and as Phizz came into the glow of the candle-light, he called to him.

"Well, Gunner, come and have a drink," he invited, "we kept this bottle for to-night."

"Thank you, sir," Phizz answered. I mustn't stay more than a minute, as I have some urgent messages to get through, and my lines are 'dis.' But let me congratulate you, sir, on the success of the attack."

"No, no," the Colonel broke in on his words, pressing both hands down on the wooden box that was his table; "touching wood, and *absit omen*, and that sort of thing, things have gone well enough so far, surprisingly well: but what if the Hun counterattacks in the dark, or just as our relief is taking place! Once we have got out of it, the poor old remnants of the battalion I brought in are -- a fine lot of lads, a fine lot, poor devils!" He stopped, as his thoughts followed their own line.

"A fine lot that are left, sir! I don't mind admitting I got the breeze up absolutely at one time, but these fellows, reinforcements and all went over like ——" he hesitated for the right word.

"Oh, it's always like that, Thurston," the Colonel took him up, "it is just these little one - or two battalion attacks that really give one the needle as bad as it can be, and then they go like steam: that is, if they get across at all." A shadow crossed his unshaven face; he was thinking of those other failures in front of this redoubt; and then he continued, "You will find it much less interesting in the big push to-morrow. Have you ever been over in one before?"

"Not really, sir," Phizz replied. "Those in 1915 were not the same thing, and we were observing from behind, not going over with one of the infantry waves."

"Well, you may think it is going to be exciting, but just wait and see. Instead of the concentration of to-night you have the whole thing spread out over the day, over miles of country, with each wave coming up for its own step forward, nobody feeling the 'needle' as badly as this afternoon (because your flanks are going over with you, all doing the same thing). I'm not talking of souvenir-hunters and back-area wallahs coming up past hundreds of prisoners into the old German line and thinking what dashed fine fellows we are, themselves included: or stoking up footling battle yarns from the Tommies with a supply of cigarettes. I mean for us in the line, for you to-morrow. Well, here's the best of luck to you and your division."

Phizz smiled unbelievingly and went to get his orders through to Lone Gun.

CHAPTER VII

Destruction under German shelling.

Warning of impending attack –
information from a shot-down pilot - gun pits destroyed -
efforts to save men and horses.

EVEN at its worst the country of the first Somme battlefield
had a weird beauty of its own. Long irregular hills and valleys from
which every green thing had been blasted lay scorched to a dry brown
by the hot autumn sun: but were curiously relieved by other hills
which had escaped that intensity of destruction, and were covered
by idle weed-grown fields pitted here and there by chance shell
craters. The woods around Mametz and Bazentin which had been
so bitterly fought through were still dense enough to hide the grim

nastiness which the struggle had left so thickly amid their splintered torn trunks. On the far ridge from Guillemont to High Wood, and round to Pozieres, the few gaunt stumps which topped the sky-line told of a still fiercer torture of earth, but above them were rolling smoke clouds which seemed never to clear without a roaring protest from the hidden guns as they set to work again. No words could ever describe it, for all the details together are no nearer to it than a snapshot is to a galloping horse. Men who saw it find a pleasure now in looking at painted pictures of that battlefield, partly it may be because of personal recollections conjured up, but also for the grim majesty of it all as the reality comes again to the mind's eye. The rocks of Galway, the moors of Cromarty have their own appeal to the artist: the picture of that wasted battle-ground bites deeper still.

It was in one of the brown valleys near Mametz that C/XYZ had dug themselves into a position. The gun pits, roofed with a layer of sandbags so far as time had allowed, were now being strengthened in an hour's respite from firing. The Major and. Brown and Phizz were working in the hot sun with coats off and braces down, filling in the roof and walls of their mess dugout, which had been cut out from the sides of a deep dry trench. The Major leaned on his shovel and lit a cigarette. The others, rubbing their rather tender hands, found their cigarette cases too, and lolling back on the heap of dry earth where they had been working, they revelled in a few minutes' easy.

"What a topping afternoon this would be on the river," murmured Brown as he watched the curling blue smoke rise from the tip of his cigarette.

The Major stretched himself stiffly with his hand on his back. "I wish to heaven I were in good rowing training now," he groaned,

"Every picture tells a story. Try Boon's back-ache ——" Brown began.

"Oh, shut up, Brownie, you ungrateful young slacker. You ought to be ashamed of yourselves insisting on an old man like me helping you to dig this place for your comfort, not make fun of mine infirmity! However, if you lie about on the ground like that you'll have stiff joints yourself soon enough. Those fellows are working jolly well on the gun pits, considering their lack of sleep," he went on, looking across to the position.

"Yes." Phizz turned over comfortably and watched them. "Isn't it wonderful how fast you can work after about a hundred 5.9's in the night".

It was a wonderful bit of luck having nobody hit," said Brown. "It is a jolly good thing you had that splinter cover up so quickly, Major."

That pessimistic gentleman looked drily at a deep hole some ten feet across, a yard or two down the trench. "I wonder if that is the one which made you turn over, Brownie, and ask if they were shelling," he mused.

Brown looked up, and then suddenly rose with his spade in his hand. "I say, isn't that the Colonel coming up the ammunition track? I'm going to start work again to impress him as a zealous officer, before asking for a transfer to the A.S.C., what!" and he jabbed his spade into the ground. Phizz got up too and laughingly joined him.

"You two humbugs, dry up. Phizz, go down into the dugout and clear away those Vie Parisiennes and the port bottle, and put the map out. Make it look more like an office, and less like a low pub at this time of day. Be quick."

"You old humbug - Phizz." Brown believed in heavy sarcasm as a form of humour.

They stood up to attention as the Colonel came up. "Good afternoon," he called to them, panting a little, for the hill was steep, and his girth middleaged. The Major invited him down to the dugout, which was cool and shady. Inside they all sat down round the little wooden table, which just gave seating for four. Brown pulled out four glasses and some whisky from behind his seat.

"I think not, thank you, in this heat." The Colonel wiped his brow. "A little lime juice if you have it would be very refreshing."

Brown called to the mess waiter for lime juice, and rather sadly poured some of the thick ration liquid into each of the four glasses. Politeness costs an effort, sometimes, and his thirst was that of a labourer worthy of his hire--not to be wasted on lime juice.

"Well, Osborne, I'll get to business at once, and I'm afraid it is not very good news I'm bringing.

You heard about that Boche plane surrendering to one of our men and being shepherded down intact into our lines yesterday afternoon? Well, the Boche seems to have been rather a poor specimen and has allowed our Intelligence wallahs to get a lot of information from him, besides what they found in his papers and maps. First thing this morning, I was sent for to the Corps counter-battery office, where they had collected these things, and had had some of his photographs developed and printed. The plane had got up to register on you, for a big destructive shoot."

The two junior officers grinned merrily at this narrow escape. Their thoughts had not leapt ahead.

"How have we been spotted, sir: did they say?" asked the Major. "I thought we were pretty well hidden."

"I asked them that myself, Osborne. They did not know definitely, but they showed me something of how it is done. Have you heard of 'sound ranging'?"

"I have heard of it, sir, but I know nothing about it."

"Neither did I. But apparently these people have a machine of sorts which records the noise the gun makes, and from that it is possible to work out where the gun is; and against that, of course, there is no concealment at all -- or at least they say practically there is none, other than not firing, which is naturally no solution. Besides sound ranging these corps counter-battery groups have several posts where observers work with theodolites and have special gadgets for concentrating all on the same gun-flash.

If they see any flash at all, they get you taped, and of course at night yours here must be visible. Then there are kite-balloons and air observers as well, and in addition to that, lots of gadgets for examining air photographs so that the least bit of a pit can be seen on them, while all wagon tracks slow up leading to the position. So with all these things working against us and checking each other, the wonder is he doesn't know all our positions. As a matter of fact the Corps people seemed to think he probably does know most of them; but the point is, he has obviously got a special hate for you - perhaps you have been doing him too much damage - and if you stay here you will be for it. I want to move you to-night, but you will have to keep this position until midnight, as infantry are expecting a minor attack on your front. If you will come along with me now, we will reconnoitre a new position."

"Right, sir. Brown, will you send a message to the wagon-line for your teams, limbers and all wagons to-night at twelve. You will come back here to tea, sir?"

"No, thanks, it is not on my way back. By the way, just to emphasize what an escape you have had, that Boche was to register one eight-inch how. and a 5.9 battery on you, and 4.2's were to take part in harassing fire. You wouldn't need much harassing after that," he chuckled.

The Major laughed too, and spoke of the unobserved shoot during the night which had left them unharmed. With a last order to knock off work for the day and give the men some sleep, he left with the Colonel.

"A cheery old cove the Colonel, what!" commented Brown as soon as they were out of hearing. He reached for the whisky again, and threw away his unfinished lime juice. "Wasn't that a sinful waste of a number 9 thirst" he went on. "Phizz send the men to bye-bye for me, there's a good fellow, and come back for another little drink with me".

Phizz had just settled down on his return when a signaller appeared at the door. "An officer to speak to Brigade, sir; urgent!" Quickly draining his glass, Brown walked briskly to the telephone pit at the far end of the trench.

"That an officer?" came a voice down the phone.

"Captain Brown speaking."

"Hallo, Brownie. The Adjutant here. Has the Colonel told you about the Hun who should have ranged on you? The wireless operator has just picked up from a Boche plane the same ranging call as that fellow had sent before he tried to begin.".

"Right. I'll clear the position, all but the signallers. Good-bye." Then picking up a megaphone he shouted out "Battery, Action!" The gunners, who had just turned in for a long-delayed sleep, tumbled out rapidly and jumped to the guns. Brown ordered the guns to be left on S.O.S. lines, and the detachments to double to a wood some two hundred yards to a flank, and to stay in the trench there. He sent all spare signallers to join them, and then went back to the mess.

"I say, Phizz, Brigade think the Boche is just going to range on us now. I have cleared the men to the trench by the wood, and I want you to join them and stay there."

"But what about you, Brownie?"

"Oh, I'll stay by the 'phone with a couple of telephonists."

"Brownie, why not tap into the line with the 'phone further down by us, instead of waiting here? It's odds on being done in if you do."

"I can't abandon the position without orders. Now jump along or you will be caught on the way over. There you are, now," he grumbled, as the heavy thud of an eight-inch armour-piercing shell shook the ground.

But almost at once a signaller appeared to say that the shell had cut the battery's only line, a buried cable to the Brigade exchange. "That settles it, Brownie," said Phizz; "you will have to come along now." So the remaining signallers were sent dashing away with the telephone, and the officers prepared to follow. Just as they left the tunnel they paused. Another shell was whooming in the air. In an instant they had jumped back into the trench. Looking up, Brown saw, in curious contrast to the slow periodic beat of the shell's whoom, a momentary vision of a very black disc shooting down towards them at lightning pace.

"That was a near one!" he panted, as they jumped up through a cloud of smoke and fine dust to trot at as dignified a pace as possible towards the wood. "——In the trench, just the other side of the mess, which is what saved us," he continued as they pulled up to a walk. "I'm glad we haven't to stay there, you know, Phizz. A decent 5.9 crump isn't a bad thing if it doesn't hit you, but these big armourpiercing, delay-action devils, they shake things so. Did you feel that one make your heart vibrate inside you?"

"I might have done if you hadn't vibrated on top of me, Brownie. We must arrange to duck opposite ways in future." Phizz brushed some of the dirt from his clothes.

Now a bombardment watched at close range from a safe vantage point is one of the most interesting spectacles one could ever see. A fireworks display, the methodical drilling of a rock, the laying of a gas-pipe, a practise artillery barrage - any one of these or a thousand other things will gather an interested crowd. But to hear large shells lumbering down: to be wondering just where they will go, and to see them pitch with startling suddenness and shoot up from their hole a rain of big and little clods of earth, and planks and debris, all appearing out of a seething hillock of smoke; to wait breathless for another heard round to burst, and only to feel the hollow earth rumblings which quiver round a dud; even to see actual destruction as when a house disappears in an instant behind a wonderful red cloud which drifts away leaving perhaps a somewhat more splintered building with another hole in it, or perhaps an empty space all this has a zest which nothing can equal and millionaires could not afford to indulge in privately. But when it is your own billet which you watch the destruction of, when your own guns are lying hidden beneath the smashing shell bursts, when from time to time little dumps of your ammunition go up in soft puffs of cordite smoke and you are expecting the infantry in front of you to need you and your guns and that ammunition at any moment to save them from attack --- then you begin to think the multimillionaire who should choose to organise such an exhibition would arrange those little details rather differently. And when beyond all this, as you are watching the successive salvoes of crumps dropping regularly each minute, interspersed with the quieter but even more deadly eight-inch, and then the harassing fire opens so promiscuously on top of it that a goodly sprinkling of the 4.2's cover the trench you are sheltering in - well, then you might perhaps prefer to have the more simple joys of a Brock's benefit, or Saturday night at Henley.

The anxiety was telling on both officers as they watched for each salvo, and time after time saw a burst apparently on top of one or other of the pits yet drift away to leave it still intact. He moved and sat down, got up and stamped his feet as if for warmth. Brown in a more phlegmatic way was terribly anxious too; the cheerfulness of the men, as they laughed at the fate of each other's belongings, instead of helping matters rather irritated the nerves of the two officers. They knew what was at stake for the infantry up on the desolate crest ahead, and though they cut this side of it out of their minds, they knew too what might be waiting for themselves and these men of their battery if the call came. At last something happened. The latest salvo cleared, and there was a grotesque muzzle sticking up through a ragged roof, with wheels splayed out from it like a collapsed toy cannon. A yellow grey belch of cordite smoke poured out from the exploding cartridges inside.

"That's one!" said Phizz.

"No, two," said Brown. The woodwork of the nearest gun pit was being licked with flames. They looked at each other.

"You can't; you are in charge, Brownie. It is my pigeon."

"I suppose it is."

There was no other word, and Phizz jumped up and walked towards the pit, with an eye always on the best shell-hole near him. As he heard the next salvo coming, he dropped out of the way of splinters, then walked on. There was little to do: he threw earth over the smouldering wood, jumped into the pit as he heard the next salvo, dashed out again as soon as it had burst, and went on with extinguishing the few licking flames. He saw a little water in a shell-hole near, and finished off the work with water carried in his hat. Again he jumped into the pit. He came out again for more water to make quite sure of the job; the hole was swallowed in a new, a larger one. He laughed, for the doing something had made him himself once more. Burnett, one of his signallers, ran across to him.

"I thought that one had got you, sir," he said.

"No, thanks; and it is out now. Come inside and we'll double back after the next one." They went in, and a crump burst just short, hurtling splinters through the open mouth of the pit on to the shield of the gun, and one got Burnett through the shoulder.

"Now quick, before you begin to feel it!" Together they slipped out, and with Phizz helping the wounded man, they stumbled along over the broken ground towards the wood. Burnett fell half-way. Phizz was dragging him the rest of the way, and two more telephonists ran out to help. All lay flat out of the way of the next rain of splinters, and then jumped up and dragged him in. Brown came along as Burnett was being bandaged and smiled himself at Phizz's new-found eagerness: for which the one thing needed, action and occupation for the mind, had turned up at just the right time.

And in the middle of it, the half-expected happened. Batteries behind and right and left rapped out in rapid chorus. On the sky-line two red lights floated above a belt of smoke, followed by two more, and two more. A telephonist who had tapped a temporary line on to the intact part of the buried cable called out in a cracked voice, "Brigade want an officer, sir, urgent."

"The S.O.S., Brownie. Shall I man the three guns left, with my section only? I'll go now."

"Half a minute, Phizz ——."

"You're wanted on the 'phone, Brownie, you know."

Phizz jumped the situation by a call, "Right section, Action! S.O.S.!" and ran across himself, followed by his gunners in a race on which some of them beat him. "Steady!" he called, and crouched; the eight-inch was coming. She pitched within ten yards, and throwing her splinters high over his flat body, seemed nearly to crush head and heart with its throbbing concussion. But he settled down gamely to the mad contest of luck and probability. Three heavy shells at least every minute, and a scattered series of lesser ones were blasting the earth in, on, and round the battery. Ammunition had to be carried in from what dumps were left outside, to replenish the small stock inside the pits. Ducking from shell-hole to shell-hole, and then into the more or less splinter-proof pits, he kept this going and controlled the shooting with no forcing of joviality, but as far as possible with just the strictness of ordinary every-day shooting. The ordinary routine was absolutely necessary under conditions when the odds were that any one pit would soon crash into a wreck of old steel and bleeding flesh; but the mere thought of that could not find a place, for the corrector was 152, fuze 80, the range 3325 and the rate of fire four rounds a minute, alternate H.E. and shrapnel - Time, Fire! fifteen minutes more, right, re-load —— and that makes quite enough to worry about if you are not to make a mistake. Besides, the men were soon too deaf in the pits to hear the shells coming, and hardly to tell the difference between a burst and the next gun.

Very soon Brown came up. "The line has been cut again, so I can't do anything down there," he said. "There's enough here to keep both of us going, too." So they stayed together, Brown looking after the guns, and Phizz the ammunition. By now the shelling and splinters and smoke had settled into a part of the atmosphere; they would duck instinctively, and rising at once, carry on at the exact point they had stopped. But after an intense hour of it, there seemed to be a change in the shelling. Brown asked Phizz if he didn't think a lot of the 4.2's were going dud, when a new scent caught his smoke-dulled membranes. "Gas," he called, and slipped on his helmet. There was an unpleasant lull in the firing while helmets were being adjusted, and then things went on just as before, save that the carrying of ammunition meant more stumbling, and there was no attempt at talking. Then quite suddenly it seemed to dawn on Phizz that something was missing. He was annoyed, for he could not think what it was, and it seemed to make his head ache to try to think. He tried to curse a man for dropping two shells as he tripped up, but nearly swallowed the gas mouth-piece instead. A muffled spluttery voice which might have been Brown's reached him. "Haven't they stopped, Phizz?"

Well, so they had. That was what was missing. The gas shells were still falling more or less harmlessly, but those ear-splitting crashes, the whizzing splinters, had dissolved, and left a blank. And our own firing on either side was slackening too. Each gun report now seemed almost a relief as it broke into that wild buzzing of the ears which was silence. Now one came to notice it, it was nearly dark. A sergeant came up, saluting, a weird figure in blackened shirt sleeves and gas helmet, to say that the gunners would need lamps if they were to continue. There seemed to be no more activity forward, no signal lights, and Brown told them to pack up and clear up from the gas shelling, 'for a breather.' When all were clear, the two officers followed. They were looking at the broken entrance of the mess dugout on their way past when with a single-minded promptness they dropped into a hole which had been part of the tunnel.

"Damn him !" mumbled Phizz. "I guessed he would send a parting shot like that." Without further lingering they crossed to the wood.

The sergeant met them again. There were no rations left intact, no water for tea, and now in the relaxation everyone had realised that he was very hungry. Now that it was all over, the last thing either officer wanted was something more to do, but there was no help for it. From a neighbouring battery, to which Phizz and the sergeant trudged, they reaped a harvest of bully and a little tea (which was limited by the shortage of water), and besides that a lot of unnecessary sympathy. The latter was discounted by their Samaritan's insistence on a history of the occasions on which he had been shelled. He offered supper to Phizz, but things were too pressing to stay with this battery to eat it, so he took it with him in his pockets and his flask.

Brown met him on the return journey. "Phizz, the Major is wounded," he said.

"H——! Not badly, Brownie?"

"No; very lightly. He is being made to rest in the dressing station, but will be back to-morrow with only a stiff elbow. I also heard from Gurney, up with infantry. The Boche made a big local counterattack to recover the Switch Line, but we have driven him out again and snaffled nearly a hundred prisoners."

"Good! But what about the new position?" Phizz asked as they sat down to eat in the trench, near the telephone.

"I am going out to find it. I have the mapreference and I will get back to guide you by midnight. It isn't much of a place, from the Colonel's account - no shelter at all, and we couldn't keep the men up a third night digging. So we shall have to stay in the open until to-morrow night."

"Curse the man who started counter-battery work!"

"Yes, this is a bit different from the days of pip-squeaks once a month, isn't it? And yet we have had amazing luck. Nobody would believe it possible, for that concentration of far more than a thousand well-ranged shells to plough up every inch round us like that, and only do in one gun and one man. Well, I'll get along now. Get things ready as far as you can, and I will meet you at midnight by the latest."

"So long." Phizz too got up to gather the men for the preparations for leaving the position.

The night hours passed very slowly. The men were not depressed, rather the contrary, but at the same time very tired and quiet. Phizz was thinking over those hours of the afternoon, wondering whether they seemed to have gone by with the speed of a dream, or to have filled the time like the passage of years. It was one or other, he was not sure which. He was interrupted about eleven o'clock by the sharp report of a couple of little whizz-bangs, or 14-pounders. They burst loudly somewhere near the guns, but no splinters flew. Just to satisfy himself that no harm had been done, he pulled out his torch and walked across. A few gunners were calling out for a light near the end pit.

"Nobody hurt, is there?" Phizz asked.

"Think so, sir, in here. Have you a light, sir?"

Phizz flashed the torch inside. The smoke was too dense to see anything, but a man in the pit was humming an old nursery rhyme-the one about ' Simple Simon.' Stepping carefully inside, Phizz found a wrecked gun, one gunner with his head horribly splintered, another with his leg almost off, and the sergeant badly gashed also and humming in his unconsciousness. They had been packing the gunstores and cleaning up the piece; the sergeant held an electric torch still in his hand, which flashed from time to time as he sighed. It was the last touch of ghastliness.

"Stretcher party at once!" called Phizz. "You, Malone, run down to the dressing station in the valley, and ask the doctor if he can come up here for urgent first aid."

He knelt down to see what he could do, choking down the fumes which stuck in his throat. Another gunner came in to help, and outside an increasing group was gathered, when some voice called, "Number Three has been hit as well."

"What's that?" Phizz jumped up and pushed outside.

"Yes, sir; just the same way. Sergeant Marryat and Wood and Lemming are killed just like that, sir."

"Impossible!" he cried, and hurried over with his torch. Other lights had been brought now and a man was inside the pit with a siege lantern.

"Aye, they're dead all right." The man was speaking without

emphasis. "Give us a hand, mate, and let's have 'em out. Oh, I'm sorry, sir, I didn't see it was you. A fine mess they've made, and fair done in the gun."

It was too much for Phizz. He felt he must laugh, must laugh aloud at the ghastly pranks which Chance had played them that day. The fumes were choking him, suffocating him, blinding him. He must get out, get away from this.

"Can you do anything for Sergeant Piggott, sir? We think he's going."

He carried on.

CHAPTER VIII

Ending in disorder.

Thurston returns from leave - finds the front line in disorder -
the Hindenburg Offensive - a desperate stand
against the advancing Germans - wounded and sent to hospital.

How many scores of times has a too conscientious amateur stage manager ruined the least chance of getting across with a bad performance, by stepping in front of the curtain to interrupt with apologies for its defects? And yet always the temptation is irresistible.

Time flies, and we have come to the last scene: yet how much of the tale of that long drama remains untold! What shall we choose from that heroic residue before the curtain falls? The author casts his mind back: back to the gallant futilities of the first Spring of the

War, Festubert and the "S-Bend" with its thick yards of impenetrable wire, the paltry allotment of bad shrapnel for the hopeless task of cutting it, and the pathetic price that England paid: or again to that desperate "Victory" of Loos (perhaps the only battle of which English War Literature could show a tale that those who took part in it can read more than once): or thence to those hammer blows on the Somme and the tragedy of the tanks in High Wood that came so near to magnificent success, and, missing it, became the centre of the thickest slaughter along those miles of gallantry; then the monotony of the winter's warfare of attrition in the devastation before the Hindenburg Line, or the swamps of Ypres, broken by the brilliance of the capture of the Vimy Ridge; again that long drawn out struggle through the mud to Passchendaele, opening so magnificently from Hill 60 to Wytschaete with the triumphant bursting of mines dug and defended through months, almost years of fighting against odds: continued against every last weight and chance that fate could toss into the scales against us. There is a gap then, of idling in the comfort of a British Red Cross Hospital, while the Division played its part in that perfect little victory at Cambrai, and the swift counter-stroke that swamped it. Then comes up again the wintry monotony, to break with Spring into hectic days of the retreat of 1918, wondering and guessing in vain at what was wrong, in despair at the muddle and the lack of grip, amazed at the enemy's failure to walk through the doorway he had so astoundingly opened, knowing only this, that it was sure to be all right in the end, because it was always thus with England. So one comes to the halt, with backs to a wall at last, and the Staff drifting forward again from the distant fastnesses to which their first rush back had carried them. Meanwhile there had been mixed days of acquaintance with troops of our gallant allies, intriguing enough, but perhaps not always printable. Then comes the swift denouement, the great advance to victory, watched by the author as a spectator from the top of Kemmel Hill, as the guns flashed through the drizzle and darkness before dawn, from Houthulst Forest to the La Bassée canal; carrying on over the swift recapture of familiar ground at the hill-foot, or with a rush through Menin and Lille and Courtrai, until with moderate cheers and quiet thankfulness we looked one sunny morning across from the flat monotony of slag heaps and mining villages, up to the green slopes that stretched from Mons, and that was the end.

Which scene shall it be? All the world knows that the easy way to success is the happy ending. And yet, this little attempt to reproduce what war felt like from one day to the next in the forward line, should surely be faithful to that life in its last act. The crowds who painted London red on Armistice Night perhaps saw the happy ending. But how many men who went into the trenches through those years came out of their .little bit at last with banners up and bands playing? Mons Stars and "1915" ribbons were thick enough behind the line, but were not so thick in front.

That is the author's apology for a scene which will bring down the curtain for Phizz at the hour when it actually fell, the darkest, before the dawn. His apology for not attempting a scene of one of the greater battles has been hinted at already, in that he could not make of any one of those few isolated days an interesting picture, because to those taking a part in them, they were less impressive than more frequent, more ordinary, more concentrated incidents of daily War. Let the War Correspondent tell of the battles, out of the mouths of soldiers, who never lie: believe me who have censored letters at the Base!

Getting married on leave may not be a disease, but at least it was a very contagious infection whose symptoms developed with alarming rapidity, and were always unmistakable. With Phizz they came to a head with the happier augury of comparative slowness: a slowness that his battery commander was very grateful for, although (be it admitted) he lost a not inconsiderable bet when Thurston came back from his last leave of 1917 still a Bachelor. However,

158

when in the early Spring of the following year, ordinary leave was suspended, the suppressed fever mounted to a rapid crisis. His application for special leave to attend to his interests in the coal and shipping trades was composed and edited by the combined literary talent of the whole mess: the result must almost have persuaded the Army Commander that on his getting this leave depended the stability of all England's commerce. Phizz then retired to the security of the wagon-line, to await the answer and the longed-for slip of yellow paper.

It came, and the Major rode over with it from the battery position. Phizz decided to set off at once, and get out of reach of any cancellation of it. They rode along to the rail-head together, setting out to a volley of cheers and friendly back-chat which anyone who knew men would have been proud of. Over dinner together at the Officers' Club, Phizz talked hard about nothing at all, to show that he was not preoccupied and dreaming.

"I suppose it is no use giving you Punch's advice," laughed the Major, as he stood up to go.

"Afraid not, thanks," Phizz answered cheerfully.

"And I shan't leave an address that will find me if anyone does try to recall me from leave before it is over."

"Right-ho! But I say, Phizz, don't get it extended if you can avoid it. Things look to me as if we should want all hands on deck pretty soon; and the men know you, and all that. With poor Gurney gone, and Brown gone to command B Battery, you know how it is. So many fellows in your circs. would contrive to go sick on leave. I'm not asking. you to promise at all, but try not to, if you can," the Major wound up lamely.

"Rather not, Major," answered Phizz. "Thanks so much for wangling the leave for me at all."

"Not a bit, it's a pleasure - leaves me one higher on the roster for ordinary leave. Now the very best, old boy, and happiness, and no troubles but little ones, and all that sort of thing. Cheer-oh!"

"Thanks, old thing! You'll see me a fortnight on Monday, Major: Cheer-oh!"

But the Major did not see him on Monday, or for many moons after. Phizz had taken little interest in the bad news that the home papers had to make the best of during his fortnight at home, and hardly appreciated the tense air of gloom he met on disembarking at Boulogne. The German hordes might be smashing through whole Army fronts, the channel ports might be seriously menaced, but he had pleasanter things to fill his mind. As an old hand at returning from leave he skilfully avoided the disembarkation authorities, railway transport officers, and folk of that ilk, and went to "jump" a lorry at the top of the hill out of the town. His luck seemed to be in, and he got a lift in an empty box-car running all the way to rail-head. Here he arrived in the afternoon, and stepped down into the familiar market square: familiar, but how changed, from the sleepy inactivity that had always seemed an inseparable part of it. Anxious crowds of civilians were clattering in every street, and thronging round the steps of the Mairie. Farmers and wives and daughters stood beside their clumsy carts, with their great grey Percherons between the shafts sweat-dried and tired, and lean cows tethered to the cart-tails by their horns. A stream of lorries was forcing a way through the confusion. Some scores of men in khaki were hanging about the Square, amused at the quaint turnouts of this crowd of refugees; with rations organised behind them, and billets and pay to be had wherever the chances of war took them, it might be easier for them to see the funny side of it, than for these anxious peasants, cleared from their houses with what few possessions they could put together, leaving behind them home and property and livelihood. Perhaps the thing that first impressed Phizz with the seriousness of the position was the scowling hostility of these refugees to the khaki uniform. He went into an estaminet and overheard two women speaking to each other in an inner room.

"And we, we had to leave the pig and the chickens and the beautiful mahogany bed. But we shall go back now. The facteur knows for certain that the French troops are coming to take over the line here, thank God. So now we go to return." It was part of a flow of gossip, without thought of an English listener. It made Phizz really think.

In all this rapid development of disaster, what had happened to his own division? Were they still there, or had they been moved? The sensible thing of course was to go and ask the local R.T.O., but then he would have to explain away his failure to do so in Boulogne, and certain regrettable experiences had made him distrustful of back-area officialdom and all its works. Anyway he had only four miles to go to the old divisional headquarters, and he would either find them still there, or learn their whereabouts and "lorry-jump" his way to them after a night's rest. He set out. As he put it himself afterwards, "Having already made such an ass of myself, I thought I might as well go the whole way." To begin with, he got a lift on an infantry limber-wagon; but the narrow pavé road was congested with the straggling refugees, dragging clumsy hand-carts, or driving creaking farm wagons, or laboriously pushing tiny barrows - (yet none so small that it was not topped with the inevitable best mattress, to add its ludicrous incongruity to the sweating labour of pushing it along in black "Sunday" clothes capped with that marvel of unshapeliness, the rustic Frenchman's best black hat); road discipline was never one of their most striking virtues, and in the surliness and stress of those bitter days it was well-nigh impossible to make headway against the tide as it flowed down the ordinary two-cart-width country road. After a desperately slow hour of it, Phizz got down and walked.

He met increasing numbers of infantry stragglers, all with the same tale of a broken battalion and the Hun at their heels: although there was no slightest echo of rifle fire within hearing, and only some fairly hot firing over Bailleul to show that a battle was being fought at all. It was not demoralisation, but pretty advanced disorganisation, which the men foolishly exaggerated in excuse of their position as retreating stragglers. They confirmed Phizz's fears, that his division had been withdrawn to "somewhere down South," or "to Italy" or what-not. Yet still he trudged on, to find someone in authority, some artillery command to give him more definite information, rather than turn back with the tide to get the same thing. At last, to his relief, he heard the hoarse cough of a couple of howitzers from the field near the road ahead, and saw a third gun being dragged across the ditch from the roadway to join them. He walked on more quickly, and went up to the subaltern who stood watching his last gun. Wearily and disinterestedly the latter answered Phizz's questions. No, he did not know where Phizz's division was: he would be only too glad to know where his own division was. No, they could not put Phizz up for the night, unless he joined them in sleeping in the open field: all their personal luggage was with their missing gun, in what was now Germany and if the Boche had had half his wits about him, the three they had somehow or other dragged out would have been there too. No, there was no chance of any battery wanting to make use of Phizz's valuable services temporarily, pending his getting to his own unit: there were only too many gunners wandering about without guns as it was: look, was there any other gun or battery to be seen or heard firing anywhere within miles of them! What was there in front of them? Well, he believed there were some of our infantry, but that was what the Battery Commander had gone to find out: meanwhile they were shelling the cross-roads near their old position, for they knew the Hun was at least so far. He walked off up the slope after his gun, haggard and yawning; but a less worried man than Phizz, for at least he had his job and knew what he had to do.

Well, best go just to the top of the rise, and see what there was to see, and then tramp back. He got there, and by the bridge at the foot of the forward slope made out a closed Daimler halted with its head to the East; a staff car, so it must at least be safe to go so far, he reflected ironically - perhaps worth while to go down and just see if he could get any change out of its owner.

Arrived there, he found a young infantry Staff Captain swinging his legs unconcernedly on the bridge parapet, with a miscellaneous two or three dozen men lounging under the trees a few yards away. Phizz explained his position.

"Good, you are just the man I want," the other replied promptly. "You are no use as a gunner now, of course: and I badly want an officer for this batch of stragglers I have collected here. You can gather as many more as come along, and then get forward at dusk."

"But I don't know the least thing about infantry command," Phizz answered, and stopped, slowly realising that now, fatally and inevitably, he. was 'right bang up against it.' This officer had nothing to do with his own division, nothing to do with him. One can guess how his mind slipped back to the parting of a short 48 hours before: went forward to that broken line ahead, with men raked together from the highway and byway, to a victorious enemy with his guns and machine-guns, outflanking them on the south, advancing now through Bailleul on the north.

"Oh, never mind about that," the staff officer interrupted him, and looked at him more slowly. "By the way, weren't you up at Corpus before the War? My name is Leigh, of St. John's."

Well, that settled it: "an awful blighter, what I remembered of him," Phizz explained afterwards; "used to write some sort of rubbish and make speeches, and punt about on the Cher with dubious females. Couldn't back out in front of that sort of fellow, however much one wanted to."

For a few minutes they talked casually of mutual acquaintances, smoking cigarettes from Leigh's tortoiseshell case. Then Phizz asked; "I say, this really is serious, is it? I want to get back to my own crowd as soon as ever. I can, unless you really are up a tree here."

Leigh got up and strolled out of ear-shot of the men. "My dear Thurston, Army Headquarters have gone back to Lumbres, fifty miles if I guess the distance rightly. The low lands and the canals from Calais to St. Omer and Aire are being flooded, and you know what that means. Even in 1914 they never actually began that. But the water only rises eight inches a day. My division was brought up here, after being smashed to bits with the Fifth Army, to this 'quiet part of the line,' to recuperate. You can guess what happened, broken battalions, raw conscript drafts, the 'Portugooses' running away, the Boche through on both flanks. There are now only scratch parties and odd units to hold up the Hun here. If he walks through, and up Kemmel ridge, he cuts off every man in the Ypres salient. As it is, the line has been drawn back there, giving up almost every yard of the Passchendaele advance. The Brigadier is out forward trying to patch up a fighting line, and I have to collect stragglers into some sort of trim, and send them in to help. The men are all right, if they are officered, but that is just what is wanting now. Yes, it is serious enough, Thurston."

"Right-ho, then, but give me a map if you have one; I would rather have a map than a revolver in these circs., and I have neither."

"Sorry, I haven't a spare one," Leigh replied; and then after a few detailed explanations, left Phizz in charge and turned the car to go round to the main road, a mile to the south. "Good-bye and the best of luck!" he waved back, and was gone.

Phizz turned to the waiting group of men and picked out a sergeant to line them up. They were a mixed lot, mostly North Country infantry, but including a couple of gunners and a stray Expeditionary Force Canteen hand. "Squad, 'tntion!" he called: "Form fours, form two deep, stand at ease!" These were the only infantry commands he was sure of. Then he coughed nervously as he realised that there would have to be some sort of a speech to get the men in hand. He took off his trench coat to gain a little time, and when he turned back from laying it on the bridge coping, he could feel a perceptible clearing of the uncertain atmosphere. "The only time I have ever been glad of having these," he told me later, with a laughing glance at the ribbons on his tunic.

"Now look here, you fellows," he began his speech, "there isn't much between us and the Hun, but the Australians are coming up to-morrow, and all we have to do is to hold Fritz up till they get here. Your division has a good name, and so has mine; so we'll play the game together. And you know," he added, with his eye on the Canteen man's deliberate awkwardness, "there will be only one way of dealing with a man who doesn't play up. Right! now, sergeant, you and your men picket this bridge, and rope in all stragglers within sight. You two gunners take this Canteen man as cook, and go to the estaminet ahead there to scrounge a good dinner: there are chickens I can see for instance, and anything else you can find. No drink whatever will be touched till I ration some out myself. The two men on the left will come up with me to the top of the hill to reconnoitre."

The sergeant reminded him of the need for picks and shovels or anything else for digging; also for extra ammunition if any could be found. The little hamlet ahead of the estaminet had once been his battalion transport lines, and he suggested there might be a chance of finding something there. So four more men with a lance-corporal were sent up there to search for what they could get, and then Phizz walked off across the fields with his two orderlies. On the crest of the hill was an old farm facing west, and from an upstairs back-window he searched and re-searched the plain in front of him for any sign of life. With the trained eye of an old observer he turned his field glasses on house and road, ledge and field and tree. From Kemmel Hill past Bailleul and round to the broken chimneys of Armentieres in the distance, the plain was as peaceful as the United States. Enemy artillery doubtless were being rushed forward, our own artillery on the move or out of action, or husbanding its ammunition supply until it was sure of getting replenishments.

Infantry and machine-gunners were out of touch with the enemy. Only the lowing of an unmilked cow, the protesting squeal from an unfed pig, broke the stillness of those deserted miles. Search as he would, he could pick up no glimpse of khaki at all: if any of the British Army lay in front of him, it was lying very low, and "sayin' nuffin'." A long three miles away he saw some small parties in field-grey stroll without apparent object over the fields between two unknown villages.

In the circumstances Phizz made up his unorthodox mind to masterly inactivity and a good night's rest. He had no inclination at all for skirmishing about with a scratch pack at a loose end in country whose paddocks and concealing flatness were ideal for advancing troops. By daylight he would try again to get in touch with someone, and if he then failed, just dig in on a little belly that he marked down in the plain, giving a fairly adequate field of fire. It was dusk now, and he returned along the east until he reached his road. Here he found a man at last, a Franco-Flemish peasant, still working at levelling the pavé setts of the roadway.

"What on earth are you up to?" asked Phizz in amazement. "You know the Germans are coming along?"

"Ah yes, and I must finish before they come," replied the old road-mender, still mechanically working his long-handled implement." It is piece-work, you understand."

"Piece-work, what do you mean?" Phizz queried again.

"From the estaminet of the Three Horses, to the kilometre post, it is forty francs - when it is finished, the piece-work."

"But whoever employed you has gone, and the Germans are coming: who do you suppose will pay you the forty francs now?"

"But the British will pay, of course, always they pay honourably. That is why I must finish before the Germans come," the man answered simply. "When it is done, I return to my home in Hazebrouck."

Phizz shrugged his shoulders and left him to it.

As well teach logic to a Hyde Park orator as remonstrate with a Flanders peasant. He reached the bottom of the hill, to find his little force grown to fifty-two, who yet were proving as singularly incapable of dealing with a little old Frenchwoman as Phizz had just proved with his road-mender.

"I a spy, you dirty English cowards!" she spat out at them. "I a spy, whose son fought at Fort Vaux and died, but never turned back to enemy yet!" To Phizz who coming up from the rear had seen so many aged figures, bent and wearily pushing the pathetic salvage of their homes away to the unknown, the situation was clear enough; but he said nothing while the sergeant explained how she had refused to stop, and objected violently to any searching of her barrow-load, with such abuse of the English Army as could only betoken pro-German sympathies. Then he apologised to Madame.

The sorely-tried old soul burst into an even more embarrassing flood of tears at the few kindly words in comprehensible French. But at last Phizz was able to get some information from her story. Her cottage lay half-way to Steenwerck, and all the previous day she had watched little parties of British soldiers retreating: a few shells had dropped near and she had retired to her cellar, until in the evening German voices sounded in the house. She had come up to restrain them from damaging her furniture, and found a dismounted cavalry patrol bringing in one of their number wounded. They went on, but soon returned and took the wounded man away again.

Nothing more happened, nobody came, friend or enemy. After a sleepless night she packed up her barrow and set off. She had met no one at all, whether in khaki or field-grey, until these sentries had so grossly abused her as to suggest she was a spy. Phizz cheered her up in return with information that would have surprised Sir Douglas Haig, and she picked up her barrow and trudged gamely off again for the safe haven of Hazebrouck (which was being shelled with a railway gun by day, and bombed every night, but what of that!).

An excellent meal was ready for the men, and Phizz shared it with them, having only the extra privilege of eating the egg which one hen had obligingly laid before her execution. He posted his night picket and sentries, gave his orders for the early morning, and after settling the men in an old barn, turned in at once to his billet in the estaminet itself. In spite of the fatigue of his long and wearing day, the anxiety of his position gave him but a fitful night's rest. He had no blankets, nothing but his trench coat, and the coldness of an April night left his limbs stiff and sore when at last the sentry came to call him in the early morning darkness. The men were gathered round a fire drinking tea, and after collecting a miscellaneous sack-full of pots and pans and vegetables and a providential ham, the little force marched up the road to the defensive position Phizz had chosen the evening before, and there awaited the slow and chilly approach of dawn. It came, with that light concealing mist which in the previous mornings had so materially aided the enemy's successive coups.

Phizz could see nothing, hear nothing and knew nothing, but dare not leave the men. The most reliable looking lance-corporal had already been sent back to try to get into touch with supplies and ammunition, and with an anxious scrutiny of faces Phizz chose out ten of the men who seemed least likely to let him down. Two were sent out to the flanks to try to get into contact with other troops, if indeed there should prove to be any. The remainder were pushed forward as an advance picquet. The rest of his little force began to dig a scratch line of rifle-pits, in an arc round the contours of this bellying foot-hill. For all their weird collection of tools, they dug as men will for whom an inch too little cover may mean a bullet in the head. The morning wore slowly on. Breakfast, cooked in a little cottage on the roadside, was brought round and eaten in the intervals of hard digging, or scratching away with entrenching tools. The air cleared gradually, and the sun shone, but the plain remained as empty of signs of life as it had been the evening before.

By eleven o'clock the men were tired and stiff-backed after seven hours of awkward labour, but the semblance of a strong point had appeared as the result of it. Phizz let them ease off and waited for the next thing to happen.

It came: an officer with an orderly and one of Phizz's detached scouts approached from behind the hill. He stopped a hundred yards away.

"Hi, are you in, charge of this party?" he shouted out, waving an arm towards where Phizz was lying.

"Come here!"

It seemed a little unceremonious, but the circumstances hardly befitted standing on one's dignity, and Phizz walked across.

"Oh, come along, hurry up!" the stranger called out impatiently as he approached. "Why the devil didn't you do as you were told and come up on my flank, instead of lounging about at the back like this, a mile from nowhere?"

Phizz paused: then, "Who are you, and what do you want?" he asked curtly.

"I am Major Wimpole of the N'th Royal Blanks, and I am usually spoken to as Sir by junior officers under my orders."

Phizz gasped. "Well, I am Captain Thurston of the Royal Regiment of Artillery, and I am used to reasonable politeness from those giving me orders, even if they have had a bad time and a bad night beforehand. However, let's get on with the War and argue afterwards. Am I supposed to be under your command?"

"Of course you are," the other retorted, "as Major Leigh told you: and instead of your obeying your instructions, here have I had to search the whole countryside to find where you had dodged to. Luckily I found this man of yours straying about, and he told me what had happened to you. Now follow me with your men promptly. Your position will be on the left of my men, in front of these orchards north of Heclin. You will have to dig in at once, and have to get better work out of the men than you seemed able to do here, judging by the way they were sprawling about when I came. So jump to it, and less back-chat, or you will know about it later!"

Again Phizz gasped; one met strange people in the war, from promoted sergeant-majors to overbearing and conceited viscounts, but that class had a fortunate knack of sucking themselves firmly on to embusqué billets behind the line. Possibly Major Wimpole was one of those rudely dislodged by the recent dramatic development, and a little disgruntled thereby. But Phizz thought of this little band of his, fatigued with really hard physical work, called now to abandon it as useless, and go to do it elsewhere all over again: thought of Heclin and its orchards, with every house and hedge marked with fatal accuracy on the Boche artillery maps: thought of the German infantry advancing with the élan of victory against this flimsy line of battered oddments whose one forlorn chance depended on perfect morale. He turned back to his men with a cheery smile - and I wonder how he did it.

"Here's good news, you fellows," he said when he had called them together. "The front line has been established, and we are going in with the dismounted cavalry from Corps Troops. They have plenty of ammunition, and rations coming up, so we shall be comfortably settled in with them." Then they gathered up tools and equipment, and advanced in open line over the mile that separated them from Heclin. They were shown their position, and with less zest than before began the labour of digging again. Phizz scraped away with a borrowed entrenching tool at the side of the sergeant.

"Don't think so much of this place, sir," the latter suggested as he leaned on his pick for a breather. "Can't see more than as far as you can spit."

Phizz laughed. "Further than I can, sergeant. But these old cavalry men know what they're up to in this sort of warfare better than amateurs like us. We shall be all right here, don't fear."

Soon the Major to whose command they seemed to have been attached came along, and began another round of surly criticisms about the work done. But Phizz had had enough. "Look here, sir," he remonstrated, "if I have to hold this scratch lot together, I won't have them badgered about for nothing. If you want to take them over yourself, then for God's sake do it."

They faced each other, two men standing in the shadow of a common danger, and unlikely to get out of it alive, but angrily hostile to the limit of worn-out nerves. Then the *deus ex machina* took a hand. There was the cough of a low range howitzer, the whoop of a small shell, a pause, and then a muffled clatter from the middle of the village.

"My hat! Exclaimed Phizz. Gas!" "What! gas?" echoed the other.

"Sounded uncommonly like it," Phizz answered; then as another whooped down and spread its dirty white mist about a soft burst, "Yes, gas of some kind, right enough, and I haven't my gas helmet. Like a cursed idiot, I dodged the sweat of taking it on leave!"

"I haven't mine either," muttered the cavalryman blankly, and ran back (with a stride reminiscent of the action of a mangy draft horse) to his own unit to try the forlorn chance of finding a spare one. Phizz hurried down his line to see that none of his men were in the same predicament as himself. Luckily they were on the up-wind side of the village, and though the gas shelling continued, none of it drifted over their direction.

"Sounds close, sir," the sergeant muttered when Phizz reached him.

"What, the shelling?"

"No, sir, the guns: a couple of mile at most, it seems to me like."

"Nearer than that," Phizz replied; "it is a 4.2 howitzer, and a bare 3,000 yards away I should say."

"Then the infantry must be less than that, sir," the sergeant suggested.

Phizz made no answer, but sent across to the outhouse where the canteen man was functioning nobly as the cook, with an order for tea to be hurried up. Meanwhile artillery fire began to thicken somewhat, though to veterans of the old trench warfare it was comparatively like child's play. It was heaviest away to the south, and mingled there with the tell-tale rattle of machine-gun fire, and the irregular, amateurish - there is no better comparison - punctuation of infantry rifles. Then it slackened down, and only the shelling of Heclin persisted. The time dragged on to an hour before sunset. Then a dusty, out-of-breath figure panted up through the orchard. "Where is the officer commanding?" he called out jerkily.

"You will find him in the village," Phizz answered from his little burrow. "Nothing I can do for you?"

"You an officer? Good, you'll do!" the stranger gasped out: he had smoked more cigarettes than was good for his wind. "General Brill's orders (I am his A.D.C.): you are to withdraw at once to the line of the road through Vieux Heclin, before the Germans attack you here. Must hold on there absolutely *at all costs*, if they attack, and they certainly will. Frightfully important, at all costs," he repeated. "Tell Major Wimpole at once." He glanced across at the village with no apparent regret that he need not go into it himself, and hurried back. Almost at once the shelling lifted off Heclin and began to pass overhead - to drop in Vieux Heclin. There was clearly no time to be lost if they were to avoid an engagement with the enemy where they stood. Phizz gave a rapid order to the sergeant and ran to the village. A few whiffs of gas caught his breath, but nothing to worry about at such a time. He found (without overwhelming sorrow) that Major Wimpole had succumbed to 'gassing and shell-shock' and retired, leaving a junior Major in charge. Quickly the orders were passed down, and the first batch skirmished back through the fields. Phizz and his new O.C. walked back together.

"We shall never hold that village," Thurston muttered; "a long line of unfortified houses like that is just a shell-trap, and nothing else." They drew nearer to it; a straggling Flanders village along either side of a pavé road with irregular courtyards and farm quadrangles bitten back into the rows of trees and hedge that outlined the home pasturages. The truth of Phizz's opinion was transparent, and the O.C. decided promptly to dig in on a clear line front of the village, bending back to the road at the flanks.

Weary and dispirited, the men began work yet once again. In half an hour, as dusk began to close, came the order that the unit on their right was over-lapping them, and they must side-slip to the north-east. This pushed them deeper into the shelling. Work had to go on in the dark, with limbs too stiff to bend, hands too sore to grip. Shrapnel began to spatter up and down the road. A man was hit here, another there. None could be spared to take them back, and they knew what fate they had to look to in the morning. The evening's gas-shells in Heclin were the one bright spot, for probably they meant that the Hun would not advance into it before morning, which would mean daylight for his attack on Vieux Heclin. Meanwhile men's spirits flagged, until the open chance of death seemed better than the weary torture of digging. Phizz passed that night in a labour of spirit which Dante might have dreamed of: encouraging the worn-out, watching that those but lightly wounded should not seize the too easy excuse and pass back, doing what pathetic little he could for those that were seriously hit, wincing as each curling flash of flame licked out an instant before its leaden hail beat down to hit or miss. He said afterwards, "If there had been one more thing, I'd have sat down and given up: but luckily it didn't rain!"

So with what last bit of skill and tact and energy he could muster, driving or enticing he stuck it out.

The arms and ammunition of the wounded had been enough to equip adequately all those that were left. The enemy began to shell the village with high explosive, a welcome relief from the shrapnel, whose short bursts had been worrying this line of men in front of it. An hour before dawn should bring its inevitable attack. Phizz walked along to see his commanding officer. He found —— an empty line!

In desperate amazement, he passed along the hastily dug pits: there was no one! He searched forward: there was no one. Behind, there was nothing but the black shadows of the village houses. He called out, and there was no answer. Unable to grasp the situation, completely lost as to what to do, he hurried back to his own men, and heard the flank men's voices in low and bitter blasphemy.

"Well, I'm —— If I am goin'; Fritz can have me as a prisoner as soon as he --- well likes."

"He ain't takin' no prisoners. I'm a married man I am, and I'm goin' back as far as I can blurry well get, blank me if I don't!"

"What's up, you fellows?" Phizz called to them through the darkness.

"'Oo are you?" one of them challenged gruffly.

"Shurrup, you fool," another broke in; " it's that officer of ourn. There's an officer been looking for you, sir," he called to Thurston, "he's ordering us back now, seeing as he couldn't find you."

"Good God, he can't be," Phizz gasped: "it's a plant, a German plant! Here, stand fast till I get him ! Ahoy there, pass the word down, stand fast and call that officer to me!".

Surly voices muttered in the darkness, then a pause, and a muffled figure stumbled up from the left. "Hallo, that you, Captain Thurston?" the voice of his O.C. called out. "I had been looking for you for God knows how long, and had just given you up, and passed orders myself. We are ordered back to the drain that runs about 300 yards the other side of Vieux Heclin. I have left a fighting outpost in these houses. Come along quickly, and I'll guide you."

"But, man, how can we?" Phizz exclaimed. Through those long hours he had he fought the temptation to give up hope, and conquering it, had held his little band to the last ounce of their guts for the bare chance of succeeding in what they were giving their lives to do. Why, oh why, could the British soldier not have his chance, without being sold for nothing by blundering fools!

"Got to! Don't understand it myself, but just got the General's orders, and there you are," the other muttered.

"Blast him!" Phizz cursed with uncontrollable bitterness; then, relieved a very little of the feelings that boiled inside him, passed the order along. In silence and chill resentment the retirement began. The pale glow of approaching dawn revealed that dispirited hunch of the shoulders which meant a fight lost before it had begun. Machine-guns began to yap, down to the flank. The sergeant caught Phizz up and told him of a shell that had killed the cook in his little outhouse on the village outskirts, and - worse still, be it respectfully added - had wrecked the half-prepared hot breakfast. However, they were all too fatigued to feel the bitterness of any grievance after the first shock of it, and reaching the drain, they found it a not unsatisfactory firing line if the men knelt down in the muddy foulness of its six inches of half stagnant water. As automata rather than as men they lined the ditch.

The light grew to a cloudy dawn: the godsend of a gloomy cloudiness that meant a morning of no mist. They did not know it, but the German luck had turned.

Rifle fire and heavy machine-gunning rattled to the south. Phizz passed down the drain making his last supreme effort to hearten the little band in his command - the forty odd survivors; but very, very soon, the need and the opportunity had passed together. Over the low rise between Heclin and Vieux Heclin a few scattered shadowy figures slipped forward and dropped out of sight: then more, and more again. The shelling of the village intensified. The sharp note of machine-gunning directly towards them swept by and grew flat again: then sharpened again, mingled with others, and grew into a steady barrage. High rounds passing over the village sizzled past, a few long-range sniping shots cracked out in reply from the drain, but Phizz passed down the word for this to stop. He crept along the waiting line to speak to the sergeant - a very different figure now in the unshaven haggardness of the weary dawn, from the alert N.C.O. he had been forty hours earlier. "I wish to God they'd left us where we were, sir, first off," he muttered; "we could have done in a tidy lot of Fritzes then, instead of being stuck like rats in this ditch."

"Oh, no, we are better off here," Phizz lied. "The Huns will be absolute sitters coming out piecemeal from the village. The only thing I'm sorry for is having to leave the wounded behind like that, in the village cellars. I hope the Hun will behave decently to them."

"Lucky they are, sir, luckier than what we will be here."

"Oh, nonsense, sergeant," Phizz retorted sharply.

"If everyone will only do his damndest we can hold on here all day without the slightest difficulty. Look here, I'll bet you my day's pay to yours that we count a hundred dead Boches between here and the village at five to-night. Will you take it?"

"I'll try to get my share of them anyway, sir !" came the satisfactory reply, and Phizz crept on.

A scattered desultory fire from rifles and two Lewis guns echoed from the village. Nothing could now be seen of the field-grey line, and there was a lull. Then suddenly a hail of machine-gunning raked each window of the village houses, and the clatter of bursting high explosives grew more or less to the intensity of a trench warfare barrage. The flashes of two field guns firing direct a few thousand yards away were followed by the hurtling crash of short range shelling. The skirmishing line of Germans slipped crouching forward and dropped to cover again. Perhaps on the right it reached the village (Phizz could not tell). A wounded man ran back from one of the houses, but half-way he was hit again and fell. A few other men ran back together. The officer left behind with them in the village ran part of the way after them, probably calling them back. They reached the drain unhurt and jumped in to join the line back. The officer had disappeared, probably returned to a house in the village. Shots were being exchanged there, cracking out now and again. Fairly heavy firing began from the dismounted cavalry. There were fleeting glimpses of Germans through the houses and trees. For some unknown reason of the enemy tactics, none appeared across the open north of the straggling village, where indeed there was nothing whatever to hold them up. Then there was another lull, with only the occasional punctuation of rifle shots and a desultory barrage passing harmlessly a little too far behind them. A couple of khaki figures sprinted back from the village towards Phizz's line. A ragged volley of sniping rounds splashed round them: both dropped. Then suddenly one leapt up again, and in spite of another wild rain of bullets he raced up to the drain and flung himself in, unhurt.

"God, there's hundreds of them," he gasped.

"Here, have a cigarette, and shut up," Phizz said, crawling up to him and reaching out his cigarette case. "How many did you account for?"

"Oh, a dozen at least, sir," the man replied, still panting. "They come on fair askin' for it."

"Well, it's a pity you didn't bring your rifle then. Take the first one if any of these men are hit, and get a dozen more!"

Another lull, long drawn out. Then from the upper stories of that straggling line of houses a sudden concentration of machine-gunning and infantry fire clattered out with ear-splitting intensity.

"Snipe all you can at machine-gun flashes only, until the infantry advance; then give them hell!" The order passed down the line of crouching figures. A few shots cracked out in reply. Gradually confidence grew as the men began to appreciate that to take aim and fire from the cover of the bank was not certain death. The machine-gunning got appreciably wilder. Germans appeared from the near side of the houses. "Now steady, but give 'em all you can." Hurrah, the welcome boom of some eighteenpounder battery, but firing alas to the right. Oh, if only he could switch it on here, what glorious execution it could do! Yes, if!

The Germans had disappeared, thank goodness. Phizz spotted the flashes of an active machine-gun, and hurried to his one Lewis gun to have it tackled. The enemy stopped abruptly, just in time for the Lewis gunner to empty his last drum into another batch of Huns. They were held, and dropped to earth. By the sound of things it must be part of a long frontal attack, extending away to the south. Huns began to crawl forward. Phizz's men sniped with spirit, but the deadly fire from the upper stories told, and told heavily. Oh, the irreconcilable need for caution and fatal danger of slacking off!

"Snipe at the windows, men: infantry only if they rush!" But the advance had stopped, here at any rate. The men were playing up better, though ammunition was beginning to be a bit of an anxiety now. A single man, all he could spare, was sent down the drain to the cavalry with an urgent request for help. Shrapnel fire began again, apparently in accurate and unobserved, but occasional rounds beat down and took their demoralizing toll. Yet the men were used to the short distances and heavy concentration of trench warfare, and stuck it well. Tediously long it continued, then quite suddenly stopped. Another swishing burst of bullets, and the grey line was leaping forward. One man reached within twenty yards, when Phizz dropped him himself. The others were held: perhaps cowed by the nerve-racking overhead closeness of their own supporting fire, some crept back. Some successfully daring sniping, and from the creeping figures some jumped and ran. "Give 'em it, lads." Yes, they were beaten off again. "Now steady, save your ammunition.

Again a lull, and time to do something for the wounded: so pitiably little in that tetanus infested drain, but yet a desperate something. Scouting round, Phizz found a little off-shoot of the drain with the shelter of a few sparse bushes, leading back as far as a hedged orchard. What lay beyond he did not know, but at least once reached it was temporary concealment, and there might, if

Providence were kind, be something further beyond it. A desperate chance, crawling barely half-hidden along that filthy little ditch, but still - he sent those of the least badly wounded to try their luck.

And now they were about at the end of their tether. Suddenly again, without a preliminary intensified barrage, batches of Huns slipped forward, dropped, slipped forward again. They were covering their own advance with deadly steadiness. Still the little band of survivors struggled to reply, and somehow or another in a last desperate rally had held the nearest batch down to a fold in the field a rough eighty yards away. And then the shadow of the end came. On the right, moving slowly and dispiritedly with hands held up, over the top of the drain there showed the heads of men making for the village: and on those heads were British shrapnel helmets.

So the Huns were in the drain, and nothing could save them now. Surrender? Ah, he was too tired to think it out, knew that his instinct would not let him take that fatal step; nothing but to wait doggedly for whatever happened. Curse, one of his own men on the outside had bolted forward in surrender too. A rifle spat out, and the man dropped; none followed him.

Crash, and crash, and crash again. It seemed as though the rending cracks burst spontaneously from the surrounding air. Dazed, Phizz saw the Huns in front jump up, and run. He picked up his own rifle, and in the act of aiming, realised that he was intensely surprised, so surprised that he could not fire - the Huns were running *back to the village*. Crash, and crash and crash again, and now Phizz knew what it was: those close range enemy field guns whose open flashes he had seen in the attack on the village, had moved round, were blazing at clean point-blank a short thousand yards away, to blast them out of existence, out of the way of the advance.

Perhaps they did not know that their little hornets' nest was already turned in the flank along the drain, and only knowing that it had contrived to hold up this extremity of the attack, were going to make sure of it in this way. Meanwhile, by arrangement or in fear of rounds which crashed at such high velocity that only an experienced veteran would know even from what direction they came, the Hun infantry had temporarily recoiled.

Ah, well, a respite anyhow! Crash, and a warmth in his thigh; he looked down, saw the long rent down tunic and breeches, and the soaking blood, felt in that instant the smarting pain of it. It made him dizzy: curse it, would he faint or not? He could not help slipping down into the water. He was swimming now, swimming, swimming. (I think he saw a face beside his, a face that he had kissed that short four days before, but he did not tell me this.) Yes, it was nice to go swimming again, but the waves made a rotten booing in one's ears. . . . . Someone was dragging him down: pulling his shoulders down under. He must fight for it, race for it, trudgeon stroke, Australian crawl . . . . .

"Say, mate, guess your mother pupped a darn fool when - hullo, the bloke isn't dead; who is he?"

"Can't say: we only got roped in together night before last."

"Gaw blimey, think you're out for a V.C. or what? When I saw you worming up that drain with him stuck flat on your back, I thought you must be like those ——s they jawed about down at our Sunday School, David and the other bahstard. Christ knows why they didn't shoot you fifty times over.

They must have been so damn interested in them shells that they couldn't see two ——s in Sydney."

"Oh, he made it safer for me from splinters, and I had a hunch that they wouldn't snipe so long as them machine-gunners didn't. They're the blokes I hate."

"Well, what are you going to do with him now?"

"Can't you give us a hand, 'Aussie?"

"Can't, sergeant! Our lads are just over the ridge, and coming up to counter-attack any minute now, and I gotter watch here. Push him behind that straw stack, and our bearers will pick him up when they come by. You can't get him back till night anyway. What are you going to do yourself, sergeant?"

"If you'll give us a drink, mate, I'll stop and see him through. Got a fag, too? Thanks. Yes, I don't know who he is; not one of our lads, but a nice-spoken young fellah. Blimey, yes, and he owes me a bet too; got to see him through now!"

A laugh, and again oblivion that ended with the slow rumbling of iron wheels - a hospital train. Phizz does not know so much as the name of the sergeant, to whom he still owes not only his life, but also eighteen and sixpence.

Chapter IX

War comes to an end.

Thurston on convalescent leave and the Major doing a staff job both contemplate returning to the front – the war ends.

IN THE OUTSKIRTS OF MONS.

———

WHOLE BRITISH FRONT ADVANCED.

The following telegraphic dispatches have been received from General Headquarters in France :—

SUNDAY.

9.17 A.M.—Our advanced forces are keeping touch with the retiring enemy on the whole front.

Our troops have occupied the Faubourg de Bertaimont, on the southern outskirts of Mons.

Farther north we are approaching Leuze and have taken Renaix.

7.55 P.M.—South of the Sambre, our advanced troops have reached the Franco-Belgian frontier.

North of the Sambre our progress has been continued against somewhat increased resistance from the enemy's rearguards. Our advanced detachments are pushing forward south-east of Mons, and have reached the line of the Canal west and north-west of that town.

On the railways east of Maubeuge great quantities of rolling-stock have fallen into our hands.

Extract from the London Times 11th November 1918

THERE is a story, probably apocryphal, told of a first night at a theatre not very far from the Haymarket; when the curtain fell on a rotten play, to the painful silence of an audience wondering whether to hiss or not, one lonely voice from the gods raised its plaintive call of "Author!"

"Author, author!" it called again.

"Oh, shut up!" bellowed back a disgusted pittite. "Shurrup yerself! I want to throw a brick at him!"

Well, dear reader, here the advantage is mine.

You might perhaps ask for your money back, but you can't throw bricks at me! I need not even borrow Shakespeare's dodge and send one of the cast forward to say my say for me in the Epilogue. With the courage of security - and, by Jove! - how brave one can be in an armchair! it is like the glorious feeling of being able to outdrive Wethered when swinging at a ball that is not there - I step forward with my best first-personal bow.

I got my leave in August, a few days later than it had been promised, and could only afford the one evening in town before catching the midnight train North. From Boulogne I wired to Phizz to meet me for dinner at the Berkeley, but the last time he had written to me was before going to a convalescent hospital, and it seemed unlikely that the telegram to his home address would get to him in time. I sat waiting in the familiar ante-room feeling the discomfort of a creased dress-suit: the loneliness of recognising not a soul in that War-time crowd where once I could have spoken to perhaps one man in four: the irritation of uncertainty as to whether I should have to dine alone, and what to do with myself afterwards. The early diners had not yet come out, the late ones had all gone in; it was twenty minutes after time, when a girl hurried in from Piccadilly, as lovely looking as -- well, of course, after many months in Flanders, one is not a critical judge, but she was one of those women who seem too beautiful to be true, until you see they really are. Her glance round the ante-room swept icily over me, and she passed with her cloak still on her shoulders into the dining room. In half a minute she was back, and sat down. I had had my third sherry, and fifth cigarette, and could not face another before dinner; with nothing else to do I watched her, perhaps stared rudely. There was something vaguely familiar about her that eluded every effort at recollection. The war had lasted a long time, my savoir faire with women was never of the best, and my courage failed at the thought of going up to ask her where we had met. Then it chanced that fidgetting with my coat I felt something hard in the inner pocket, and took out a real pre-war golden sovereign put there heaven knows when or why, to survive the half-dozen times the suit had come out of my box at the Club since 1914. Idly I tossed it up, and even while it hung in the air said to myself, "If it's heads I'll go and ask her!" It fell, Heads. I caught a glimpse of an amused glance as I stood up and put the coin away. Then Phizz came in.

"Hullo, Major, old man, haven't you begun yet? You must be famished!" He strode up to me without a trace of a limp, then - "I say, Molly" (turning to the cloaked girl), "however long have you two been sitting here like this? My wife, Major, but how on earth did you fail to recognise each other!"

"I am so sorry," Mrs. Thurston smiled at me, "you poor man, you must have got dreadfully impatient waiting about like this. It was so stupid of me, but your photograph is in uniform, and I expected you to be in uniform, and so I didn't think it could be you at all at first. Then when I half thought it was you, you hadn't recognised me from my photo that Fitz said you had seen, and you yourself looked - well, different somehow."

I led the way to our table. "How, different?" I asked rashly.

She hesitated, thinking probably of my baldness, which a uniform cap conveniently hides; then quietly, "Less happy: eh, more stern," she said, and continued with a laugh, "the result of being kept waiting for dinner, of course!"

The waiter was re-arranging the table for three instead of two. "You won't mind giving Molly dinner as well, will you, Major?" Phizz asked.

"Not at all, delighted! Stupid of me not to have thought of it!" I blundered through stammering apologies for my own very discourteous lapse in not having mentioned her in the wire.

"You see, she opened the telegram, and tried to telephone to me at the hospital," Phizz explained, "but I did not get back there until after seven. Then I had to chase round the countryside to find the doctor and get leave, and I was short of petrol too. At best I could not help being late, so I asked her to come along and hold the fort and keep you going till I rolled up. It really never occurred to me, somehow, that you could fail to spot each other. You still have to make your excuses for that, Major," he added with a grin.

"Yes, and you'll put your foot in it with Fitz" -- (videlicet Phizz) -- "if you are rude about the photograph, which he used to swear was a jolly good one; and with me of course if you are rude about the original!" added Mrs. Thurston.

"I -- eh, well, evening wraps and things, you know! and perhaps you too have changed a bit since it was taken."

"How?" Mrs. Thurston asked, enjoying my embarrassment I fear.

"Well, eh - more happy, less stern," I returned, and plunged on, "but really, you know, I was just coming up to ask you if you were not you, so to speak, when Phizz blew in."

"So that was what you were tossing up about, was it?" she asked smiling.

"Oh no, certainly not, not at all!" I stammered again.

"Then it must have been whether to give Fitz up and go and feed," she rejoined. "A real golden sovereign, wasn't it? Do show me it," and the conversation turned. We talked of many things, of the battery just a little - at least I remember discussing the old battery gramophone, and who should have it now that none of us remained there -- but mainly of plays, and politics, and people at home. After the peaches there was one of those embarrassing pauses when small talk has given out.

"You're looking a bit off your oats, Major," Phizz broke the silence; "cares of a wearing life at Army Headquarters? How do you like the change?"

"Not much, Phizz," I replied slowly; "to tell you the truth, that is worrying me a bit. You know, I might just as well be in a top floor in Mincing Lane with a typist flapper and an office boy, for all that my job seems to have to do with the War. And my Mess bores me rather: none of the fellows has been in the line or seen the War at all since Mons, and none of them wants to; they sometimes make me rather sick with their talk about it. They hang around all day fighting on paper, and dash off after dinner lest someone senior should ring up before they are back to ask if plum and apple jam has pips in it; in the intervals they jaw about the long and wearing hours of Staff life, and how it compares with trenches for hardship. You know the sort of thing!"

"Yes, it must be rather feeding," Phizz mused, "but - you're not proposing to do anything, are you.

"I don't know, Phizz: when you left me to go assing around with the infantry as you did, I was the last one left, the last one of ourselves, so to speak; and it wasn't frightfully bracing. Three years of it had taken the pipeclay off the traces too, and spoiled my young enthusiasm for shells and rats and muddy blankets. Besides, you know how it was settling down into a mechanical business, shoved here, pushed there, ordered to fire on this and not that, exchanging guns, taking orders about ammunition, stuck with new officers and new men from God knows where, seeing the horses about once in a blue moon! No; it wasn't like the old days."

"I am thinking about going back, too," interjected Phizz quietly.

"Good Heavens, but that's out of the question, Phizz. What about ——". I stopped abruptly. Women may be an insoluble mystery to back numbers like me, but we can at least see when two young 'uns are back-teeth awash with a healthy devotion. There are lights in the eyes that don't need William James on Psychology for their interpretation.

"You see, my medical board will vet. me for 'light duty' if I like, the doctor says; and that means I could get into my uncle's works under the Ministry of Munitions: I am his heir you know, and he wants me to go. But if I press them to pass me fit for France, they will do that of course: there is no limp or anything left at all. I gather the battery isn't quite what it used to be, Major. I don't want to go back to it alone.

But —— Phizz glanced up at me. "Yes but ——": ever so slightly I had bent my head towards his wife; yet she noticed it and interrupted quickly.

"When Fitz and I decided not to wait any longer for the War to finish, we also--eh, decided, that it should make no difference to his — to his sticking it."

I think again of her face, strained with an intensity of proud self-control which I had seen before: seen where all the paraphernalia of Army regulations and discipline and tradition and decorations were needed to call it up, all the excitement of action to keep it from breaking, and the fatal inevitableness of disaster in the alternative, as the final prop when all else began to go. So at last I learned that the finest courage that England had to show was not recorded in the "Short Stories of Brave Deeds."

"And so, if Fitz can go" — the words came with that crisp lightness at a vital crisis which Shakespeare interpreted by particularly painful puns - "I think he will"

"If you go too, Major, that settles it," said Phizz.

Slowly I felt in the bottom of my pocket for that sovereign, a George the Fifth, I noticed. "Let's toss for it," I said.

§

Who on that August evening knew or dreamed of the astounding denouement which September and October were to bring? Not, apparently, the politicians, pathetic in their futile pretences that all was well and they were not wrangling with each other: not, certainly, our general staff, as I would illustrate if it mattered to the story: not, least of all, amateur soldiers like myself. For years I had watched the heaving struggle of that Titanic front, had seen line after more formidable line grow up behind it, with trench and strong point and impenetrable hedge of wire: had admired (as I still am not ashamed to admire) acts of courage on the German side which would have made some of our own units proud, and were indeed sometimes mentioned in our G.H.Q. dispatch itself. I had enough of science in me, too, surviving from Oxford laboratories, to appreciate the marvellous ingenuity of invention which (*pace* the possible exception of poison gas) British, French and American combined did not surpass. I had enough technical knowledge of artillery to wonder, and wonder still, at the effectiveness of some German guns, discounted as it was by unimaginativeness in the direction of them. Yes, if I had been sent to follow Joshua in a seven days' tramp round Jericho, I should not have been more surprised to see its brick walls totter to crumbling ruin than I was to see that mighty bulwark of Germany collapse as fatally. What gave way was not the realities of fact, but those subtler, more essential realities of character and morals, and he who can estimate those is a prophet, and not plain man.

And how could I foresee that motor jaunt from Army headquarters to the old battery, which I took with an embusqué confrère a bare ten weeks later. Kitty, my little mare, had been ridden into a ringbone by a lout of a twelve-stone subaltern more fit to be in a knacker's yard than a commissioned officer in a horsed unit. Beauty had been "cast" and shot, God knows why. The battery commander was the first man I had recommended for a commission - yes, the irony of it!-because he was a useless peace-time sergeant whom I could get rid of in no other way: now, promoted in the helter-skelter of second and third line units in England, he had at last come out to France to command the old battery. The band, with its piano and violins, had been scrapped for "lack of transport" - lack of transport! when that most precious part of all our stock-in-trade had survived Cambrai and the Albert retreat. The men - but why go on?

§

The tossing of a coin two feet high, and its fall again: only an incomplete fraction of one second! I watched the glint of light on its fateful spin, while two thoughts turned over and over as rapidly within my head - the discomfort, the monotonously cruel danger to my own skin; and again the sacrifice that Phizz was offering himself for, and his wife, after what they had stuck already. The sovereign fell and I covered it on the back of my left hand.

"Heads we go, tails we don't," said Phizz quietly. The waiter stood at my elbow: perhaps even in war time money tossing was not a nightly introduction to the Berkeley. Phizz was looking at his coffee cup. Mrs. Thurston had her clear eyes fixed on me.

"Tails it is," I said quickly, and slipped the sovereign to the waiter. "A double Justerini for me quickly, and you can keep that as your tip. Jove, it's hot!" I wiped my brow.

"Thank goodness that's settled," said Phizz, with a sigh of relief. "England, Home and the Munitions Factory for your obedient servant! I could do with a brandy too, Major."

"I'm sorry, Phizz," I apologised; "what about you, Mrs. Thurston?"

"No, thank you, I will leave you together for a few minutes," she replied, and rose to pass into the lounge. I looked into her face, as I stood beside my chair: her eyes, unfathomable, gazed straight at mine: mine fell, and she was gone.

Unfathomable? Yes, they seemed so then, but ten weeks later, as again that crucial instant came to my thoughts, I knew that she had seen: seen not the sovereign before I slipped it to the waiter, but seen through me.

The sovereign had fallen Heads!

Glossary

ASC	Army Service Corps
Blighty	Soldiers' slang for Britain
Deus ex machina	Latin for god from the machine, meaning a happening of fate
DSO	Distinguished Service Order
Estaminet	French, a bar
Gamp	A reference to Sarah or Sairey Gamp, in Dickens' Martin Chuzzlewit. She was the stereotype of the ignorant and unreliable nurse before Florence Nightingale's reforms.
GOC	General Officer Commanding
GSO	General Staff Officer. GSO 1 usually a Lieutenant-Colonel
HE	High explosive (in this context)
Hugo	Victor Hugo (1802 – 1885), one of France's best-known writers, poet, playwright and novelist, known in Britain for Les Miserables and The Hunchback of Notre Dame.
Kubelik	Jan Kubelik (1880 -1940) a Czech, son of a gardener, was a well-known classicalviolinist and composer, who first played in London in 1901 -02. One of his sons was Rafael Kubelik, the conductor.
Minnie	Soldiers' slang for German *Minenwerfer* or trench mortars
MO	Medical Officer

Mr Hardy	Hardy's, a famous anglers' supply shop in Pall Mall, London, first opened in 1897. It nearly went under in the 1960s, but though no longer a family firm, it flourishes as The House of Hardy
NCO	Non-commissioned officer
OC	Officer commanding
OP	Observation Post
Parados	Covering earth wall, to protect from enemy fire
PBI	Poor Bloody Infantry
Percheron	Flemish breed of heavy drafty horse
QMS	Quarter Master Sergeant
RA	Royal Artillery
RND	Royal Naval Division
RTO	Rail Transport Officer
Sisyphus	Character in Greek mythology. A delinquent king, who was punished by being condemned for all eternity to push a heavy boulder up a hill, only to have it roll down again.
Toffee Apples	Slang for 60 lb mortars
WD	War Department
Wethered	Roger Wethered (1899 – 1983) a famous amateur golfer who won the amateur golf championship in 1923. He was called up into the Royal Artillery in 1918, but discharged very shortly, on the Armistice. His sister, Joyce Wethered, Lady Heathcoat-Amory (1901-1997) is regarded as the most brilliant British woman player of all time.
VC	Victoria Cross, the greatest award for bravery.
Verey Light	A flare from a cartridge ejected from a gun. The flare lasted for about 15 seconds and gave a quick impression of the enemy lines.